T0106125

# A RECORD OF TRACES AND DREAMS: THE HEART SUTRA

BY: KIDO INOUE

Translated by
Doiku Takeda

Edited by
Reggie Pawle, Ph.D

iUniverse, Inc.
Bloomington

# Record of Traces and Dreams: The Heart Sutra

*iUniverse books may be ordered through booksellers or by contacting:*

*iUniverse*
*1663 Liberty Drive*
*Bloomington, IN 47403*
*www.iuniverse.com*
*1-800-Authors (1-800-288-4677)*

*Because of the dynamic nature of the Internet, any web addresses or links contained in this book may have changed since publication and may no longer be valid. The views expressed in this work are solely those of the author and do not necessarily reflect the views of the publisher, and the publisher hereby disclaims any responsibility for them.*

*Any people depicted in stock imagery provided by Thinkstock are models, and such images are being used for illustrative purposes only.*

*Certain stock imagery © Thinkstock.*

*ISBN: 978-1-4759-4886-8 (sc)*
*ISBN: 978-1-4759-4884-4 (e)*
*ISBN: 978-1-4759-4885-1 (dj)*

*Library of Congress Control Number: 2012916589*

*Printed in the United States of America*

*iUniverse rev. date: 09/26/2012*

# CONTENTS

**THE HEART SUTRA LINE BY LINE**

SHARISHI SHIKI FU I KU KU FU I SHIKI SHIKI SOKU ZE KU KU SOKU ZE SHIKI JU SO GYO SHIKI YAKU BU NYOZE    37

*Sariputra, form is not different than emptiness; emptiness is not different than form. That which is form is empty; that which is emptiness is form. This is also true for sensation, perception, intention, and awareness.*

SHARISHI ZE SHOHO KUSO FUSHO FUMETSU FUKU FUJO FUZO FUGEN    40

*They are not born nor do they die, are neither sullied nor pure, nor do they increase or decrease.*

ZE KO KU CHU MU SHIKI MU JU SO GYO SHIKI    43

*For this reason, within emptiness there is no form, nor is there sensation, perception, mental formations, or cognition.*

MU GEN NI BI ZESSHIN NI MU SHIKI SHO KO MI SOKU HO    48

*There are no eyes, ears, nose, tongue, body, or mind; and no form, sound, smell, taste, touch, or mental formations.*

MU MUMYO YAKU MU MUMYO JIN NAISHI MU RO SHI YAKU MU RO SHI JIN    51

*There is no ignorance, nor is there cessation of ignorance. There is no old age and death, and no cessation of old age and death.*

MU KU SHU METSU DO MU CHI YAKU MU TOKU I MU SHO TOKKO BODAI SATTA E HANNYA HARA MITTA KO SHIN MU KE GE    54

*There is no suffering, no cause of or annihilation of suffering, and no path to liberation. There is no wisdom or attainment because there is nothing to attain. Because the bodhisattva depends on Prajna Paramita, there are no obstacles.*

MU KE GE KO MU U KU FU ON RI ISSAI TEN DO MU SO KU GYO NEHAN    60

*Because there are no obstacles, there is no fear. Separating from everything, from all upside-down views and from attaining Nirvana, too.*

vi

# FOREWORD

In his first book, "Zazen: The Way to Awakening", Master Kido Inoue explained the essence of Zen to attain a liberated mind and awaken us to the "Truth" of our nature beyond the ego.

Now, with this, his second book translated to English, Master Kido Inoue transmits the core of the True Dharma by explaining step by step the Heart Sutra, which is an outstanding guidebook to the path of liberation. Although The Heart Sutra is brief, it contains the core concepts of the True Dharma and the Great Compassion of Buddha. It is regularly chanted by Buddhists as a way to practice the Buddha's teachings.

To fully understand the meaning of the Heat Sutra one cannot simply follow nor have faith in what it says without detailed analysis. One should also be careful when trying to analyze its content and be aware that the Heart Sutra cannot be fully grasped with pure intellect. The mind is constantly asking "why?" provoking doubts and deliberation. Practicing the True Way requires you to throw away all things and to forget the ego. Yet, the words should be comprehended with the mind and the heart and its full understanding will naturally reveal through practice. It is because of this the guidance of a real Master or Roshi is required. Such Master is Kido Inoue who's teachings and practice are straight forward and honest. In order to master something, you have to follow a teacher you believe in and strive according to the teaching.

The teachings of this sutra are deep but subtle and describe the Ultimate Path to a liberated mind. I hope you enjoy reading the detailed explanations of the Heart Sutra by Master Kido Inoue and evoke you to practice the Buddha Way.

# INTRODUCTION

## 1. The Most Widely Recognized Buddhist Sutra

There is no Buddhist sutra more familiar to practitioners of Buddhism than *The Heart of the Perfection of Transcendent Wisdom*, commonly known as *The Heart Sutra*. Its brevity combined with its profoundness make it just the right sort of volume conducive to reading. The length of the sutra including the title is a mere 276 Chinese characters. Chanting quickly, it can be read in less than a minute. Or, reading more deliberately, it can last a few minutes. Its concise style evokes in the reader in a short period of time a sense of intimacy with its message.

The Heart Sutra was first brought to Japan by the Japanese diplomat Ono no Imoko, who returned with it from China in the early 7th century. The original manuscript Ono no Imoko carried back from China is said to be presently enshrined at Horyu-ji temple in Nara prefecture. Japan's emperor at the time, Junnin Tenno, who reigned from 733–764 AD, issued an imperial edict encouraging the nation's people to read the sutra. This decree begins by proclaiming:

> *As I have heard, The Great Perfection of Transcendent Wisdom is the mother of all the various Buddhas. Honor and recite these verses without weighing the good fortune it may bring or the merit that may accumulate. When the nation's ruler is mindful of The Great Perfection of Transcendent Wisdom, wars and calamities will never overrun the country. When the common people are mindful*

> *of The Great Perfection of Transcendent Wisdom, the gods*
> *of plague and pestilence will be shut out of their homes.*
> *Nothing surpasses the cessation of evil and the attainment*
> *of good fortune. Kindly spread the word to all regions*
> *of the country that each and every person, regardless of*
> *gender or age, should be mindful of The Great Perfection*
> *of Transcendent Wisdom throughout their daily activities.*
> ...

In 818 AD, a great plague struck the country and nothing could be done to stop it from spreading. As a prayer for the well-being of the people and the tranquility of the nation the ruler of Japan at the time, Emperor Saga, wrote out the Heart Sutra by hand. It is believed that as he wrote, he prostrated himself three times after writing each Chinese character of the sutra. The beautiful manuscripts of succeeding emperors who continued in similar practices have been declared national treasures of Japan and are stored in a special hall at Daikaku-ji temple in Saga prefecture.

## 2. Origins of the Heart Sutra

I would like to begin by mentioning some background information about the Heart Sutra. Its formal name in English is *The Heart of the Perfection of Transcendent Wisdom.* In Japanese it is known as *Maka Hannya Haramitta Shingyo,* and in Sanskrit it is called *Prajnaparamita Hrdaya.* It is most popularly known in English simply as *The Heart Sutra.* It is part of the much larger *Perfection of Transcendent Wisdom* canon of Mahayana sutras whose extraordinary size comprises 600 volumes. It is divided into three parts: introduction, main doctrine, and dissemination. Topics covered in the introduction include origin and causality. The main doctrine section explains the essence of the teaching. The last section explains how the teaching will spread across the world in order to deliver people from ignorance.

Although very short, the Heart Sutra is generally considered to contain the essence of the entire canon. There are as many as eight different Chinese translations of the Heart Sutra. The first translation, rendered by the Kuchean Buddhist monk and scholar Raju Sanzo[1], has become accepted as the standard work.

Raju Sanzo was an extraordinary man. The title *sanzo* is an honorific name conferred upon extraordinary Buddhist scholars who were well-educated in the sacred writings. In 401 AD, he was summoned to the capital of Chang'an in ancient China. He remained there for 13 years immersing himself in translating various texts before passing away. Through the work of Raju Sanzo Chinese Buddhism underwent revolutionary development. His work also asserted profound influence on intellectual thought as well as on many other aspects of Chinese society. It is believed that he had as many as 3000 disciples.

About 250 years after Raju Sanzo's time, the monk and scholar Genjo Sanzo[2] was sent to India by an imperial decree of Chinese emperor Taiso[3]. Genjo Sanzo brought back to China and translated many Buddhist scriptures and texts, including the 600 volume *The Perfection of Transcendent Wisdom*. Texts translated from Genjo's time to the present are called *new translations*, while texts translated prior to his time are referred to as *old translations.*

People attributed the safe completion of Genjo's India travels to the fact that he carried along a copy of the Heart Sutra. This is considered the beginning of the belief in the extraordinary merit to be gained from the Heart Sutra.

## 3. Genjo's Principles for Translating

During the lifetime of Ono no Imoko only the so-called old translations existed. Presently the new translations are predominantly used. Due to the high quality of the Genjo Sanzo's work new translations are regarded as exceedingly more faithful to the original Sanskrit texts.

Genjo Sanzo established his own principles for translating. He drew up five guidelines to determine the kinds of written materials that would be inappropriate for translation. They included:

1  Chin., *Kumarajiva*, 344-413 AD.

2  Chin., *Xuanzang*, 602-664 AD.

3  Chin., *T'ai Tang.*

1. Writings that embrace a variety of meanings.
2. Extremely private or confidential writings.
3. Writings indigenous to India that were not found in his own country.
4. Antiquated writings.
5. Writings that were better left in the original Sanskrit.

The first word of the Heart Sutra provides an example of Genjo's principle to leave certain words untranslated. In Sanskrit, the Heart Sutra begins with *maha.* The Sanskrit *maha* means "large," "abundant," or "triumphant." Today it has assumed the meaning "infinite in both time and space." Therefore, *maha* means "infinite" or "eternal" in a material and spiritual sense and also "infinite" or "eternal" in terms of the concrete and abstract. *Buddha* encompasses everything while at the same time transcending all things, including 'body and mind,' 'self and other,' 'large and small,' 'common and sacred,' 'life and death,' and 'good and bad.' There was no word with an equivalent meaning in the Chinese language; therefore, *maha* could not be translated. Consequently, in his translation of the Heart Sutra from Sanskrit to Chinese Genjo used only *phonetically* equivalent Chinese characters for *maha.* This is also true for the Chinese characters used to write *hannya haramitta,* as well as for the famous phrase at the end of the sutra, *gyate gyate hara gyate hara so gyate.* The characters in the Chinese translation were selected because they sounded similar to the Sanskrit words, not because their meanings were equivalent. Consequently, trying to interpret a meaning from the Chinese characters for these words is futile.

## 4. Genjo Sanzo's True Intention

It is surely a mistake to try to grasp the true meaning of Buddha's teaching intellectually, that is, by using conceptual thought. In the same way, trying to understand and master the Heart Sutra philosophically or by somehow interpreting and analyzing the meaning of the words will not help a person grasp its true meaning. In order to avoid the danger of such an understanding, Genjo Sanzo decided against simply producing a word-for-word translation. Genjo's real intention was to encourage people to devote themselves to actually mastering the Buddha's teaching. More than anything else he wanted followers to be faithful to the Dharma itself.

We should be grateful for the devotion of Genjo Sanzo. Choosing to remain faithful to the true mind of Buddha, he made no attempt to translate passages falling under any of his five guidelines. Deliberately trying to translate words into non-meaningful Chinese characters is as foolish as trying to measure the vast ocean with a thimble or trying to view the wide open sky by peering through the end of a long, narrow pipe. We should never forget Genjo Sanzo's boundless compassion and kindness.

How should you treat these untranslatable passages? The only way, naturally, is to arouse a great doubt for yourself and to thoroughly investigate. It is through your own efforts that you are able to acquire a resolution to the question, What is its true meaning?

Here is where the road divides into two paths: those fall who into conceptualization trying to understand, thereby becoming attached to words and phrases; and, those who truly practice the Buddha's teaching, meaning, they practice the teaching in order to realize and personally experience it for themselves. In short, the road separates into those who deliberately raise personal opinions based on an understanding of words and concepts, and those who put the teaching into practice by throwing away words, concepts, and personal opinions.

In order to grasp the true meaning of Buddha's teaching, one must put aside words and phrases and directly put into practice the teaching of Buddha just as it is. This is the practice of the Buddha Way and the way to realize the true meaning of Buddha's teaching. This is also the true message of the Heart Sutra. In other words, we should conduct ourselves according to the teaching of the Heart Sutra.

When our practice genuinely ripens and we penetrate to the bottom of this matter, body and mind disappear and we become one with the Dharma. This is because at the moment of realization the true condition or state of all things becomes evident. Here words and phrases are completely irrelevant.

This is likewise true for all of the sutras and other Buddhist scriptures. One does not grasp the deep meaning of the Dharma by reading the sutras. One can only arrive at their true meaning by practicing in accord with the Buddha's true intention. More precisely, one has to practice Prajna Paramita intimately. It means to endeavor day and night in practicing Prajna Paramita. This means to get to the absolute bottom of the present moment we call 'now': earnestly and simply become the present moment.

## 5. Sariputra

The Heart Sutra explains the actual way to carry out Buddhist practice. It begins with a narrative about the bodhisattva Kannon[4], referred to as Kanjisai in the sutra. The bodhisattva Kannon was giving an important sermon, and his audience included Sariputra and the 15 other original disciples of Buddha. The 16 disciples already experienced an initial glimpse into the truth of 'no self.' The Heart Sutra's teaching was to be their guide in ultimately awakening to "the mysterious state of true emptiness." In particular, Sariputra's religious practice was especially ripe, and the Buddha no doubt held high expectations for him.

Sariputra was renowned for his outstanding intellect. When he was eight years old, he travelled to Magadha, a country in India at that time, and stayed in a certain castle town. By chance, he was present when an annual debate before the king was to be held. For the debate four seats were set up on the stage. One seat was for the king, and one seat was for the crown prince. The remaining two seats were for participants. Sariputra calmly took one of the participants' seats. Expecting to entertain themselves at the expense of the child, the king and others in attendance hurled questions at young Sariputra, but to their amazement they all found his answers to be correct and irrefutable. Eventually, the king's chief debater appeared, and a great debate unfolded between the two. In front of the king, the court, and the common people of the country, Sariputra completely outmatched the king's chief debater. The king was extremely impressed. He pronounced Sariputra the wisest man in all the country and rewarded him with land. The king also appointed him leader of the country's

---

4 The Bodhisattva of Compassion; also known as Kanzeon in Japanese.

educational system. These results show how brilliant Sariputra truly was.

At a young age Sariputra experienced a glimpse into the state of emptiness. Although originally a Brahmin, he attained an initial experience into selflessness at the age of 16 by devoting himself to religious austerities. One day Sariputra encountered a follower of the Buddha named Assaji and asked him about the teaching of Buddha. As Sariputra listened to Assaji explain Buddha's teaching, he was immediately able to grasp the teaching and readily embrace it. This was Sariputra's first encounter with the Buddha Dharma, and it vastly altered his life.

When he first met Assaji, Sariputra was already regarded as an able teacher with some degree of insight into the Way. He was therefore able to perceive the tremendous depth of the Buddha Dharma as Assaji explained it.Sariputra was also endowed with a natural ability in guiding others. By the time he met Assaji, he already had one hundred followers seeking his instruction.

Sariputra had a trusted friend named Mokuren[5], a leading practitioner of supernatural powers at the time who also had many disciples. Together with by their disciples, they went to the Buddha to request his teaching. The Buddha, a genius in his own right, was amazed at the clear thinking Sariputra exhibited. Buddha praised him declaring all of the wisdom accumulated in India would probably amount to no more than one-sixteenth of Sariputra's wisdom.

Because of his outstanding intellect, reasoning power, virtuous character, initiative, and leadership, Sariputra immediately earned the esteem of the religious community gathered around the Buddha. Through Sariputra's effort and devotion the religious community quickly grew. He held great promise for realizing the Ultimate Way, and it was only natural that Buddha himself held the highest expectations for his accomplishing it. Unfortunately, Sariputra passed away during the Buddha's lifetime before he was able to receive Dharma transmission.

The Heart Sutra is a Dharma discourse delivered as though being spoken to Sariputra alone, instructing him to listen closely. Transmitting the Dharma is truly difficult, and being able to transmit

---

5 Skt., *Maudgalyayana.*

it to even one person puts to rest the greatest concern of a teacher of the Dharma.

Now it is our turn to take Sariputra's place. The bodhisattva Kannon is now turning toward us to expound the miraculous Dharma. We must listen carefully. If you think about it, there is truly nothing more precious because you are able to meet the Buddha instantly and in person. Here teacher and disciple are in immediate communion. Truly awakening to this world without the slightest room for uncertainty, you instantly become one with the Buddhist masters and patriarchs of antiquity.

## 6. The Essence of the Sutras

What is the essence expounded not only in the Heart Sutra but in all Buddhist texts? It would be nice to have a simple explanation to this question. Needless to say, all of the sutras expound Truth, and Mind. This is the essence of all of the sacred writings of Buddhism. It is also what is known as the Dharma, the Buddha Dharma, and the Way. The real nature of Truth and Mind are the issue here: it is what is called emptiness.

In the entire natural universe, of which every one of us is a part of, there are mountains and streams, grass and trees, the moon, snow, and flowers. There is spring, summer, fall and winter; and there is north, south, east and west. Things come together, and they fall apart. Things are consumed, and things flow along. There are medicines, and there are also poisons as well. If you throw water onto a fire, the fire goes out.

We are made up of mind and body. There are six sense organs: eyes, ears, nose, tongue, body, and mind. And there are six sense objects: color, sound, odor, taste, touch, and elements. There are the *four basic sufferings* of birth, old age, sickness, and death. There is delight, anger, sorrow, and pleasure. All of these are circumstances or conditions of the cosmos, and they are the working of emptiness. If you eat just enough to satisfy your appetite, you become full, and you naturally stop eating refusing any more to eat. We love and trust, and we betray and deceive. We give, and we take. We give a helping hand, and we also destroy. We seek peace, and we deliberate over committing wholesale slaughter.

This is called the law of causality. The law of causality is made up of *cause, causal factors,* and *effect*[6]. It is also referred to as the law of cause and effect. Causal factors[7] are infinite and boundless. They have no true nature of their own, and they manifest freely due to circumstances. Therefore, as I mentioned before, manifold things arise due to causal factors, and when these causal factors, or circumstances, are exhausted and used up, then what manifested is completed and comes to an end. This is known as the cycle of cause and effect. Since all things come about due to causal factors, it is known as "occurrence through causes and causal factors." Moreover, if circumstances are present, events may reoccur.

Sutras and Buddhist treatises expound the law of causality, constantly driving home the fact that all things are *non-substantial,* that is, things have no true nature of their own. At the same time, the sacred writings point out that this body and mind of ours – our existence – is ultimately due to causes and causal factors. Provisionally, we use terms such as 'simply,' 'as it is,' and 'now' to explain the condition of things as they are at the present moment. But to really understand this reality, you must awaken "the Way-seeking Mind" and clarify the reality of non-substantiality for yourself. You must liberate yourself without wasting time. Know that life is short. When you awaken to the fact that all things are empty, the world of 'no birth' and 'no extinction' becomes ours. Finding liberation from 'life and death' we attain real peace of mind. This is what the Heart Sutra explains.

## 7. Emptiness

Emptiness is the universe as it is. *The universe* means "absolute boundlessness." It also means all things. If you are talking about the size, depth, or breadth of the universe, if you are talking about something being the absolute largest or absolute smallest, or if you are discussing space and time – since all of these things are immeasurable and boundless, they are called "the universe." In other

6  Jap., *in-en-ka.*
7  Jap., *en.*

words, depending on causal factors of time, place, and so on, a relationship or connection forms between things or people. Then, that relationship is completed and ends. What occurs or manifests has no true nature of its own. Therefore, it is free to become anything in accordance to casual factors. Since the makeup of all things is simply a coming together of causal factors, their nature is provisional and non-substantial.

It is important to understand properly what impermanence means. Even assuming that the present is impermanent, it is still the present reality. This is what emptiness is. This is what is referred to as 'existing while not existing.' It is like a mirror. If conditions are met, anything can appear in a mirror, but what appears has no substantiality or true nature of its own. Everything depends on casual factors; beyond that, there is nothing. This is the proof that all things are empty. The practice of the Buddha Way is realizing this reality for yourself.

To use a seed as an example of cause and effect, the seed of a plant is the cause. Each seed has its own particular past. Moreover, each seed carries particular data and causal factors that can bear future results. However, the seed itself cannot produce a result. The seed is just a seed, as it is. But if the seed drops to the ground, the earth provides the causal factors needed; and before long, the seed sprouts and takes root. Then, when the time comes, its flowers and finally bears fruit. This is what is called the result, or effect, in a cause and effect relationship. The effect then instantaneously becomes the cause of future results.

All things themselves are the result of the law of cause and effect and are at the same time causal factors in other cause and effect relationships. Therefore, when conditions arise, without fail a corresponding outcome will result. In this way things continuously undergo constant change. This unfathomable state of circumstances is the universe. It is our daily affairs and our whole life. Since nothing escapes this law of causality and everything undergoes constant change, all things as they are now at this present instant are referred to as 'just' or 'simply' existing. This is what is called emptiness. It is what is referred to as "the Dharma," the law of phenomena arising due to causality.

The Buddha Dharma is universal truth. When you awaken to this truth, which is the reality of emptiness, all suffering and adversity falls away like frost and dew melting in the sun. You will attain great peace of mind. This is the teaching of the Heart Sutra. If you really delve into the teaching, you will understand in great detail what this means.

## 8. How Did the Buddha Convey Emptiness?

Shakyamuni Buddha spent his entire life expounding the path to liberation. This liberation is a salvation that is complete. In what way did he expound this path so that others could realize emptiness? How he did this is condensed into a concise teaching called The Heart Sutra.

As the sutra says, it is particularly important to be thoroughly absorbed in "...the deep practice of the Perfection of Transcendent Wisdom." This is *Prajna Paramita*, and it means persistently tempering and forging your efforts to get to the absolute bottom of this matter of the present moment. If you do this, your Buddhist practice will genuinely mature and you will awaken giving prooving the teachings of the Heart Sutra. You will come to see for yourself the truth of the passage, "When he clearly realized the five skandhas were completely empty, he was delivered from all suffering and pain." Buddha wanted us to realize and experience this for ourselves.

Even though Buddha clearly and comprehensively explained the Dharma, he proclaimed before entering Nirvana, "I have not expounded a single word." In other words, the True Dharma is a "mind to mind transmission" that is "outside the teaching." This means that the realization of emptiness cannot be conveyed by words and phrases but can only be acquired through one's own effort and practice. Said another way, Buddha urges us to realize that everything in the teaching is no more than a finger pointing at the moon and that we must practice exactly as the teaching demonstrates. That is the meaning of "deep practice of the Perfection of Transcendent Wisdom."

All of the *Dharma gates*[8] that have been expounded are for the purpose of each person obtaining the Dharma for themselves. They are guidelines to deepen your trust and set your focus. The Dharma can be explained through both spoken and written words, but it cannot be transmitted in the same way. Put simply, it is impossible to master the mysteries of the mind by means of explanations by others.

Why is this so? The written and verbal forms of the Dharma are processed by the intellect. Since the outcome of such intellectual activity is based on thought, ideas of understanding and not-understanding inevitably arise and sentiments of 'good and bad,' 'like and dislike,' and so on, interfere or get in the way. Since the intellect functions in this way, understanding the Dharma through words or texts can be no more than a pretext for an understanding that is based and established upon personal views.

Here Buddha taught that you must separate from consciousness, which is the root of all delusion. To do this, you must temper and refine your Zen practice. Buddha established this as the foundation of Zen practice. The way to separate from consciousness is to disregard all intellectual discretion and cease from all reasoning. In other words, Zen practice should be simple and direct. Without distraction or looking elsewhere, simply and solely endeavor in becoming one with your present reality. Becoming one with things, the self utterly disappears. When you thoroughly penetrate this, you realize the truth of emptiness.

The Heart Sutra lays out the way to realize this. It says that no matter how much you grasp at words and phrases it is meaningless. Just like riding a bicycle or driving a car, you will not be able to operate the vehicle merely by understanding the components and how they work. Other than actually getting behind the wheel, there is no other way to grasp the essence.

## 9. The Five-Petaled Flower Blooms

The appearance of Buddha could be considered mankind's most blessed and auspicious event. He was the first person to reveal the Dharma gates to liberation. This is the way to freedom from the root

---

8 Paths to the Dharma.

of all suffering. Even more joyous and auspicious is the great event that took place one day on Vulture Peak when Buddha's disciple Makakasho[9] smiled as Buddha held up a flower. This event marked the first transmission of the Buddha Dharma.

Vulture Peak is the world's most sacred mountain. The fact that Makakasho achieved liberation means he penetrated to the source of the present moment. This is truly extraordinary because he was the first person to bear witness and demonstrate that anybody can accomplish liberation if they just make the effort.

The true form of emptiness and the message communicated through liberation have been properly transmitted in the direct line descending from Makakasho to the 28th patriarch Bodhidharma. Being told by his teacher to go to China, Bodhidharma left India and arrived in China after an arduous journey. It is said he arrived in what is now Guangdong, China. About 300 years after Bodhidharma's arrival in China, the "five-petaled flower" of the True Dharma blossomed into "five houses and seven schools." The five houses were the original five Zen sects: the Unmon, Hogen, Soto, Rinzai, and Igyo sects. During the Song Dynasty the Oryu and Yogi schools of the Rinzai sect were established, making "five houses and seven schools."

In addition, the Soto Zen tradition recognizes 27 generations in the Indian lineage of the patriarchal line and 23 subsequent generations in the Chinese lineage. After receiving Dharma transmission from the 27th Indian patriarch, the 28th patriarch, Bodhidharma, went to China. This severed the line of transmission of the True Dharma in India, and Bodhidharma became the first patriarch of China. Zen master Eihei Dogen, who is recognized as the founder of Soto Zen in Japan, is the 23rd Dharma successor after Bodhidharma. Dogen lived about 800 years ago and was the 51st legitimate Dharma heir in the patriarchal line from the Buddha.

In this way the true transmission of the Dharma was conveyed from India to China, and from China to Japan. This is what is referred to as "the eastward advance of the Dharma." About 100 years after the time of Dogen, the True Dharma spread widely throughout Japan. This was due not only to the efforts of monks from foreign lands, but

---

9 Skt., *Mahakassapa.*

also because of the appearance many splendid native-born monks. Examples of some of these Japanese monks are the founders of new Buddhist sects in Japan which blossomed into the so-called "five mountains" affiliations of leading monasteries that appeared in Kamakura and Kyoto.

All of these religious leaders were great monks who dedicated their lives to the practice of Prajna Paramita, the Perfection of Transcendent Wisdom. That is, they achieved liberation through their persistent practice penetrating into the present moment. These religious leaders are referred to as "good friends and guides leading others to the Dharma."

The purpose of a reclusive monk such as myself audaciously presenting a volume like this is to transmit the True Dharma and the Great Compassion of Buddha. In doing this, I wish to highlight the fact that the Heart Sutra is an outstanding guidebook for the path to liberation and for the practice of the Buddha Way. This sutra describes the Ultimate Path in a most straightforward manner. I would like you to know that by exerting yourself daily in the way it describes the time will come without a doubt when the results of your effort will manifest.

Right now Buddha is passionately and sincerely challenging us, "Look! The vital point of dropping off mind and body is right here!" Right now, let us all listen and learn well in order to practice the Way and to bring about the rebirth of Venerable Makakasho. There would be no better way to repay our gratitude to the Dharma.

# MAKA HANNYA
# HARAMITTA SHINGYO

*"The Heart of the Perfection of Transcendent Wisdom"*

*MAKA...*

*"Great..."*

*MAKA* is the first word of the Heart Sutra. It means "large," "great," or "triumphant." In other words, it means something exclusive in size. *Exclusive* means "unique," "single," or "single-minded." It means universal power. It is getting to the absolute bottom or source of something. When you are utterly absorbed in something, there is no self. When there is no self, everything becomes oneself. In other words, this means that *MAKA* is 'no self.' Nothing is as great and powerful as something without a self or center.

I think that almost everyone has experienced at one time or another being so engrossed in their work or studies that for three or four hours they utterly forget time. In this way, they forget both themselves and what they are doing. You are so engrossed in what you are doing that there is only the activity itself. Space and time, mind and body — literally everything — is forgotten. Everything disappears. This is because during these times you are utterly one with the activity itself. There is no room or space for anything to become a hindrance or distraction. There is no gap where anything extra can intervene.

Solely and single-mindedly being utterly absorbed in the present moment we call 'now,' the self is transcended. Becoming more and more deeply absorbed in this way, the self drops off and one obtains emancipation, or true freedom. This is Buddha's awakening. Here one realizes MAKA.

However, if you are not vigilant in maintaining the Way-seeking Mind, this vitally important awakening experience becomes lost. You end up returning to old, customary habits and ways, falling into the confusion and conflict of the regular world and discarding the precious path to Enlightenment. In other words, because you fall into the habit of examining and dealing with your present condition and because you do not give up the habit of looking back at the past, it becomes impossible to get to the very source of this vital matter. These bad habits themselves are the self, or ego. Before someone has completely awakened, his or her condition is like an ongoing dream. The habits of the customary mind are truly deplorable.

Having compassion for those who have fallen into these old habits, Buddha expounded the teaching of the Heart Sutra so that people could awaken quickly from their dream. As long as the self remains, conflict with others is unavoidable; confusion and discord within oneself is inevitable. Therefore, it is necessary to awaken to true MAKA. This is done through the practice of sitting *Zazen*.

Gutei, a 9th century Zen master from China, was a unique monk. During his entire life he simply raised his finger to answer anything he was asked. There was a young apprentice monk who would mimic this, raising his own finger, too, whenever someone asked him about the Way. When Gutei heard about this, he chopped off the apprentice's finger. The apprentice ran off in pain. Gutei suddenly yelled to the fleeing monk and raised his finger. Seeing Gutei, the disciple also tried to raise his finger, but it was gone. At that moment, the young monk instantly dropped off the self and deeply awakened. He had penetrated to the source.

If Gutei had been thinking about human rights or personal reputation, if he had been preoccupied with a sense of guilt or ethical responsibility, or had he been concerned about crisis management or pain, he could have never done what he did. Because he was utterly empty he was able to act freely and unrestrained. This mind, this action, and this freedom—all arising from no self—are what is known as *MAKA*. Zen master Setcho praised Gutei saying the remarkable capacity he displayed exalted the Way. Gutei not only transmitted the Dharma for future generations of patriarchs, but he cut off utterly all vestiges of the ego and attained *MAKA*.

The apprentice monk threw away his life in search of the Dharma and experienced profound joy in attaining this boundless treasure. To be sure, the joy he experienced was no doubt more profound than the pain he felt. In addition, as an expression of his boundless gratitude for his teacher's kindness he undoubtedly devoted his whole life to utterly throwing away all worldly thoughts and cares and to living a full and unrestricted life of *maka*.

Gutei's whole life was *MAKA*; therefore, raising his finger was also *MAKA*. As Gutei was about to die, he told the community of monks, "I attained my one-finger Zen from master Tenryu and was unable to exhaust it my whole life." At his moment of death, he raised his finger and passed away. Since this *MAKA* finger transcends life and death, there is no way it could possibly be used up. And because this finger has no real or true nature of its own, it doesn't belong exclusively to Gutei. When you simply raise a finger, it instantly becomes the rebirth of Gutei.

The only way to realize *MAKA* is to direct all your efforts to penetrating the present moment.

# HANNYA...

## *"Prajna..."*

HANNYA and the more familiar Sanskrit equivalent, *Prajna*, mean "wisdom," in other words, the wisdom of Buddha. It is the activity of the egoless mind. Such wisdom does not emerge from personal opinions or viewpoints, but rather out of boundless, unrestricted emptiness. Prajna is extraordinarily pure and plentiful wisdom, the same wisdom that can feed a multitude of 100 by breaking and sharing a single loaf of bread. It is salvation.

If you are wondering what is necessary to achieve this, it is the mind of thoroughness and care, in other words, it is the mind of compassion. It is freedom from resignation and compromise. It is the mind of 'just' doing, of 'simply' being. It is the world of things just as they are, where no concerns or matters of any kind intervene. It is the kind of wisdom that manifests only when all concerns have been completely abandoned and the mind is utterly empty. This is Prajna, the wisdom of Buddha.

From the time of Zen master Tokusan[10] to his disciple Seppo and from Seppo to his disciple Gensha, the course of the Zen sect in China flourished widely during their time. They were all extraordinary and great masters. When Gensha sent a letter containing three blank sheets of paper to his teacher Seppo, Seppo reacted true to character. Seppo understood that Gensha dwelled in a state of universal peace that pleased and reassured the ancient patriarchs and masters. Gensha simply, or just, sent the letter to his teacher, and his teacher simply received it. There is no wisdom as profound as the wisdom of 'simply.' For those who have reached and realized the Way, it is a transmission between minds, a communion of mind to mind. It is a communication without relying on words. The wisdom of Prajna is the mind detached from 'time and space' and separate from letters and words.

A child will sleep soundly when not bothered by things, but when it becomes hungry or when something goes wrong, it lets us know by just or simply crying. Even admonishing the baby to stop crying has no effect on the baby's crying. The crying is neither a conscious

---

10 Tokusan is presumed to have lived around 850 AD.

need nor a personal desire. It is simply the action itself. This is the wisdom of non-discrimination. This is the world of 'no self'' and the wisdom of uncontrived spontaneity. It is the condition of the universe just as it is, which cannot be manipulated or interfered with by any person or thing. It is what is known as Prajna.

If you penetrate to the bottom of this matter, the self is forgotten, and mind and body become one. Salvation is the moment of great awakening. It is the moment of returning to one's true mind of non-discrimination. The wisdom that unfolds and radiates at this time is Prajna, the wisdom of Buddha. This is the heart and mind of Shakyamuni and the heart and mind of all the various Buddhas and Patriarchs. It is to dwell in a state of universal peace. The essence of the Heart Sutra's teaching is to become utterly empty, to throw away everything, and to simply be this reality of things just as they are in the present.

Buddhism explains there are three kinds of Prajna: the written word, contemplation, and ultimate reality. But the present moment 'as it is' is not concerned with explanations. Those people who are committed to putting the teaching of the Heart Sutra into practice should endeavor exclusively in the Way, leaving behind words, and throwing away all reasoning. Those who have penetrated the Way reach or attain *Paramita*, which is explained next.

## HARAMITTA...

### "*Paramita*..."

*Paramita* is usually interpreted as meaning "perfection," "to reach the other shore." In other words, it means salvation, or freedom from suffering. Salvation exists since delusion and suffering exist. Assuming that delusion does exist, in regard to it there would naturally be the teaching of the path to salvation, or Enlightenment. So it would become a matter of crossing from this shore of delusion over to the other shore of Enlightenment. Although this reasoning seems logical enough, there is a pitfall here we must be careful of; that is, What are delusion and suffering?

Aren't they after all just conditions of ordinary life? When you are eating, for sure there is nothing but eating. Looking at eating more closely, when you hold your chopsticks or fork, there is merely the holding of the utensil itself, and when you pick up food there is only that action itself. Then you bring the food to your mouth and chew the food bite by bite. All of the ancient patriarchs and all of us here perform this activity in the same way. In a word, this is what is called eating. "Now I pick up the chopsticks; now I pick up the food; now I bring it to my mouth." These actions vary respective of time, and the activity itself changes accordingly. In the actions themselves, however, there is only total emersion in the present moment. Please be very careful about this point.

Both the present moment and the working of cause and effect have no substantial reality or true nature of their own. Therefore, there is nothing that binds or restricts us. Accordingly, we act freely and without restraint no matter what the circumstances may be. Moreover, since all things themselves are reality as it is, there is no delusion or enlightenment apart from it. Therefore the truth of the present moment, as it is, is already manifested. There is no deluded way of eating, nor is there an enlightened way. Since at each moment there is only the reality of the present moment, there can be no 'this shore' of delusion and no 'other shore' of enlightenment.

A long time ago someone wrote:

Delusion is this shore,
Satori, the other shore.
Being attached to neither.
Nirvana is things just as they are.

This is the meaning of Ultimate Reality. It means that in the present moment itself everything is complete just as it is. Each moment is just causes and causal factors themselves and the present reality just as it is. Already, things simple exist in the present moment just as they should. That is why Paramita is called ultimate reality. What matters is whether or not we clarify this for ourselves. The world of Zen is endeavoring to penetrate the present moment. When this becomes clear, it is called Paramita.

What must we do in order to be able to enter the world of Zen?

Since Paramita is already our true nature, we must avoid trying to become, reach, or attain something. Simply thinking about it or trying to attain it is called *worldly passion*[11]. It is an obstacle to penetrating this matter.

The present moment is already Paramita. You only have to realize this truth for yourself. Not being able to realize it means there is an obstacle in the way. That obstacle is the ego. It is the gap between mind and body. You need to return to your original nature of "mind and body are one." In order to awaken to this oneness of mind and body, you have to constantly persist in endeavoring to become the present moment. If you devote your wholehearted concentration without distraction to becoming the present moment, the time will come when the gap between mind and body melts away and both merge into one. That moment is truly like awakening from a dream where all karmic hindrance collapses. It is the moment of the arrival of salvation and the resolution of this great matter. But if your efforts are directed somewhere other than in penetrating the present moment, you will become lost and stray away from the True Way.

There was once a monk earnestly seeking the Way. His aspiration for Enlightenment was unfaltering. Before he awakened to the Dharma, he was lamenting one day about the poor state of his practice. Seemingly out of nowhere an extraordinary mendicant appeared before him carrying a staff and wearing a straw hat. It was the nun Jissai. She was a very impressive priest who had practiced under the severe instruction of Zen master Ganto. Seppo was a famous disciple of Ganto, and she herself no doubt trained hard, too.

Jissai came in and walked around the surprised monk's meditation cushion three times. Then she stood straight and tall at the entrance. There was no self, no priest, no meditation cushion—simply the Dharma itself was standing there. The monk was astonished, but he said to the nun to take off her hat in deference to the sanctity of the meditation room.

---

11 Jap., *bonno*

Jissai said, "I will take off my hat if you say the right word. If not, I will leave." She was saying that if you are a real monk, make a greeting that will make the patriarchs dance with delight. If not, I will leave immediately.

He could not say a thing. As she turned around and was about to leave, he offered, "It is getting dark. Why don't you stay overnight?"

Jissai repeated, "If you can say a word, I will be happy to stay."

She was saying , "Tell me what the Dharma is. If you say nothing, I will leave". In the end the monk had nothing to say and Jissai left. For someone like Jissai who has reached the Way, the mind ground is as perfectly free and clear as the Western sky, and nothing can intrude.

Nothing is as great and powerful as someone who has forgotten the ego self. Heaven and earth become our body, and all space becomes the mind. This is the mind ground that we reach and achieve. This is exactly what Paramita is.

After the nun left, the monk felt terribly ashamed and in self-rebuke said, "I have the form of a man, but I lack the spirit needed to be one. I will leave this hut in search of a true master to begin training over again." That night he dreamed he would be visited by a great Dharma friend.

Before long, Zen master Tenryu appeared, and the monk greeted him with great respect. Tearfully the monk related the whole story about the nun who visited him. Upon hearing his story, Tenryu held up a finger. The time was ripe: this time the monk's practice was fully mature. Simply and single-mindedly seeing Tenryu's finger, the monk became one with it. Forgetting the ego, he profoundly awakened. For certain, this one raised finger dispelled all of his doubts and testified to the great compassion and wisdom of Buddha that the nun Jissai was trying to communicate to him. Undoubtedly he gratefully burned incense and reverently prostrated himself in gratitude to his teacher Tenryu.

The monk in this story is none other than Zen master Gutei, who cut off the finger of the young apprentice monk. This experience of dropping off mind and body is called Paramita. It is the difference between reaching the other shore and not.

## Mind

*Karida* is the Sanskrit equivalent of the Japanese word *kokoro,* meaning both "heart" and "mind." The meaning of *karida* is highly significant. *Karida* is what makes a plant stand up without collapsing. It signifies the center of all things. Everything has a center.

Then, what is man's center? It is Mind. What is the center or essence of Mind? It is the true mind, the original mind, which is egoless and free of opinions.

However, there is nothing more elusive than the mind. Its form is unfixed and cannot be grasped. At the same time, we cannot separate from it. Ceaselessly functioning, it becomes angry and then sad. It admires and then deceives. Its miraculous form truly is like an apparition. Therefore, it is no easy matter to awaken to its true form. The reason is that it has no substance or true nature. What is referred to in Zen as "the great matter" is to master or realize that things have no substantiality or true form of their own.

Briefly departing from the main topic, allow me to explain about the mind in a little more detail.

## The Usual State of Mind

When people recall an unpleasant past experience, the unpleasant feelings relating to the experience instantaneously arise regardless of sentiments, wishes, or intentions. Usually, all of the information we obtain from past experiences accumulates in our heads. However, the make-up of the mind itself is greatly influenced by many factors, including genetic factors and things like experience, environment, and individual effort. In particular, parents, home environment, and human relations are factors that determine the course of a person's life.

As this accumulated information or data encounters certain conditions or circumstances, it impacts all areas of the mind at once. It arouses various concepts, thoughts, images, and so on; and this further sets in motion a range of sentiments and emotions.

Saying it another way, since our minds are always ready to respond, almost instantaneously a chain of complications of diverging complexity are set off all at once. In terms of sheer volume and speed, it is far beyond the control of the intellect or even the power of one's own will. Since this habit of the mind linking thoughts together one after the other is thoroughly integrated and entrenched, it is terribly difficult to manage. It is what I refer to as the habit of the ego.

This is why a person can lose his or her presence of mind in a moment's time and fall into confusion and discord. Since this is the state of the ordinary or common mind, there can be no peace or comfort.

Let's now try and untie the entangling components that comprise the process of thought.

## The Three Elements of Intellect, Feelings, and Intention

### 1. Intellect

Simply speaking, mental activity can be divided into three components: intellect, feelings, and intention. These mysterious and unfathomable mental functions are not always present but appear instantly according to time and circumstances. As human beings, these three elements are essential. Lacking even one of them would have serious effects.

As human beings, our most remarkable attribute is our intellect. The intellectual range and capacity among people varies immeasurable. Moreover, it is not simply a matter of assuming that the sharper the intellect the better. A wicked person's intellect will be used for evil, and the more sophisticated the evil mind is the more wicked will be the evil created. Sadly, such functions as personality, social development, and moral character are not all found within the make-up of the intellect. If they were, higher intelligence would bring about more sophisticated character development. But since this is not so, we humans run into problems.

In short, the intellect is similar to a computer that processes information subject to a person's will and convenience. Undoubtedly, a clever person will find this convenient and advantageous. However, because the intellect lacks the ability to reflect on itself or to feel sympathy for others, and because the intellect holds no beliefs or ethical values, it would be very dangerous to place absolute trust in the intellect. No one who lacked such values as moral principle, faith, trustworthiness, or sense of responsibility could be considered compassionate and humane. Neither could anyone assume a person of sharp intellect to be free of worldly passions.

The early Zen masters from both China and Japan knew well the pitfalls of man's intellect and feelings. Through the actions of their everyday lives these masters showed us how to conduct ourselves in such a way to avoid succumbing to the unforeseen difficulties arising from them. The early masters' outlook of religion was nothing special or unique. The very principles governing their daily lives were themselves their own religious beliefs:

Do only good;
Abandon all evil.

These two lines sum up the Buddhist idea of morality. In Japan these principles were taught by temple priests and handed down generation after generation as character-building ideals. They served as both religious and character models. They have been the underlying spirit stressing an ideal way of life teaching the value of diligence and virtue. It is sad and frightening that we are now losing sight of these ideals.

## 2. Feelings

Feelings are what carry out these principles for living. Feelings are man's emotions, sentiments, and sensibilities. They are called by different names, but all of them are what we generally refer to as "feelings." They are indeed an important factor in what a person is. If it were not for feelings and sentiments, life would not be worth living. A person is said to possess reason or good sense only when his or her intellect is substantiated by moral principles, trust, and faithfulness. Human feeling and sensitivity fosters various sentiments, such as grace, serenity, and joy. Because of these sentiments life becomes rich and precious to us.

If we lacked these sentiments, life would be dreary. People wouldn't care if they lived or died. Life would lack meaning, enrichment, and real feeling. If there were no feelings or sentiments, we would have no home, family, spouse, or friends. Society as we know would not come into being, and the human race would not exist as we know it.

Why? Because without compassion and love, man and woman would not bond, and without affection parents wouldn't feel a parent's endearing love for their children. Without this affection, child-raising would be impossible and humanity could not continue.

If there is an intrinsic difference between feelings and the intellect, it is that feelings are directly linked to energy. In other words, feelings are inseparable from mind and body, and they are connected with the force of life. Love is both energy and a life force. It is actually due to the power of true love that one can genuinely teach, watch over, and reprove those we foster. When love is lost, that energy is lost, too.

However important feelings and sentiments might be, they are truly a double-edged sword. The energy capable of love and compassion is also the same energy capable of driving someone to do something equally terrifying when love is betrayed. When someone flies into a rage, their mental state can assume a physical manifestation that prompts impulsive behavior. This energy can become reckless and impossible to manage. Since this reckless energy is based on the instinct for survival and self-preservation, it can become aggressive and violent.

On the other hand, this energy is also the driving force behind risking bodily harm for the sake of defending moral principles, beliefs, one's family and country. Because these sentiments exist, the seeds for such actions are always present. It is why wars and genocide never go away. The disquiet in the world is due to this element of feelings and sentiments. In extreme circumstances, destroying your antagonist may seem to be the only alternative in order to save yourself or those close to you.

*The Pine Wood Corridor Incident* of 1701 in Edo Japan is one notable example of this. In this famous story forty-seven samurai warriors threw away their lives in the name of revenge after their lord was forced to commit suicide. In distinct contrast to this story, the life of Makabe Heishiro demonstrates to us how the humble manservant of an ill-tempered master could establish a place among the ancient masters through diligent Zen practice. Makabe Heishiro was able to transform the energy of humiliation and anger into "the

Way-seeking Mind." These two examples demonstrate how human feelings are intimately linked with the force of life. The energy in these two examples is the same, but the core of the matter is making the best use of it.

Since ancient times philosophers, men of religion, and thinkers alike have exhaustively explained in lofty detail the various disciplines of their respective paths. Fundamentally, though, they are simply talking about how man can control his actions and behavior. In other words, they are detailing a practical methodology for controlling man's animalistic energy and life force. A beautiful mind is tempered by forthrightness, sincerity, and honesty. It is in constant self-reflection and is inspired by beautiful thoughts and reasoning. For this kind of mind to blossom, a rich reserve of human warmth and kindness must be nurtured. This kind of mind is most effectively fostered in the home by someone of similar spirit and in a setting of uprightness and simplicity. In this modern age we are always trying to avoid all hardship and suffering. However, the spirit to challenge and overcome hardship is important, and this frame of mind is necessary in order to really live happily. We tend to think that a strong mind means a strong will, but preceding this there are feelings and sentiments that establish the orientation or predisposition of the heart and mind. These feelings and sentiments are a person's beliefs. These beliefs are the reason why someone with a beautiful mind will demonstrate a strength seemingly far beyond his or her own capability when the occasion demands.

### 3. Intention

Intention, or will, is an important function for properly controlling the intellect, feelings, and one's behavior both in public and in private. When this facility is strong, healthy, and consistent, work goes smoothly and efficiently. A person who is able to lead by example and to promote common goals for honest intentions makes the kind of capable leader that is sought after today.

In contrast, a person whose actions are selfish will always create problems and conflict with others due to their self-centered outlook. As a result, they cause trouble and are shunned by those around them. Intention stimulates sentiments that moderate the maligned tendencies of the intellect. It is also an invaluable mechanism that can act based on scientific reason, thereby preventing reckless tendencies of the intellect and emotions. A basic premise of man is endeavoring to maintain the general peace and to promote the common good, and one's intentions should at the very least heed to this basic assumption without succumbing to self-assertive behavior. This is a way of saying that actual intention controls even the basic beliefs from which convictions arise.

Here is an example of something often seen all over the world. While living in another country, people may understandably identify with their native ethnicity. However, if they persist in harboring an view of the world based on individual ethnic attitudes and beliefs over and above the history, cultural traditions, education, and other practices of the host country where they live, it will invariably cause irreparable conflict instead of building a foundation for assimilating into one's host country.

We tend to think that a situation such as this is a matter for the intellect. One tends to think that being reasonable or rational would prevent such problems from arising. However, if you take a look at reality, you will see that what is constantly taking place throughout the world today does not actually take place within the realm of the intellect. Although it is true that the element of feelings does hold enormous influence, what makes the difference when making up one's mind is how scientifically based one's intentions are. There is a danger that the intellect tends to serve personal interests. This is because the ego is at the root of decision-making. What controls self-interest is the individual's basic intentions. Basic intention means placing self-interest last. In the case of an expatriate, he or she needs to set aside personal preferences and follow the basic norms of the host country where they reside. The process of assimilation goes more naturally and smoothly when all people involved share common basic principles in aspiring for a brighter future.

In order for intention to function in a healthy way, it is essential that it be deeply linked with a sound intellect and level-headed feelings. The healthier each of these three factors are, the more natural and healthy the relationships between these will be.

What is truly sad is seeing a person becoming overly self-assertive and willfully combative in a need for self-fulfillment. This only makes everyone around uncomfortable. Or, in discussions involved in a decision-making process, someone aggressively tries to push through personal ideas in deciding the matter. This only creates stress physically and mentally. As a consequence, things do not go smoothly and the situation is aggravated instead of being resolved. Maybe there is sufficient understanding of the situation and enough determination to resolve the issue, but if someone gets sidetracked by such sentiments as dislike and ill will, the three elements no longer function together harmoniously. The result is a person is unable put his or her whole heart into their work.

Intention also means to manage your feelings and get any preliminary preparations in order so that you can go about your business in a reasonable manner. Intention is what simplifies and streamlines things. Intention gets rid of unnecessary mental activity and supplies the energy to wholeheartedly endeavor in the activity at hand. The proof of a sound will is healthy feelings and a healthy intellect.

## The Trilateral Relationship

The trilateral relationship between intellect, intent, and feelings is very important. What are commonly referred to a person's spirit, character, and disposition are mental workings that take shape based on the integration of intellect, feelings, and intent. It goes without saying that each of these factors has to be fundamentally sound. Furthermore, this union is not fixed. At any particular time, their degree of integration determines the quality and content of the person's actions and the individual's degree of stability. In other words, the more harmoniously integrated and non-exclusive these three elements are, the better. This is because each of the elements functions depending on the performance of the others.

The three elements should work together harmoniously. For example, "Certainly this is good. This is something that promotes the common good and will benefit the future. Above all, as a human being it would be the proper thing to do. Let's cooperate and do what we can." That is how intellect, intention, and feelings act in harmony.

There is no conflict whatsoever, and work goes smoothly. An able person, a person of character, conducts him or herself in this way.

As an additional benefit, if these three elements function harmoniously, you can live life confidently in a state of equanimity and composure. You are spared from worldly strife and discord because there is no unnecessary thinking, no evil intent, and no indecision. Naturally such things as anxiety, a sense of lack, and feelings of dissatisfaction have no basis to arise. There is magnanimity, gratitude, and a sense of wholeness. Such a person naturally follows a way of life based on moral principle and trust.

In contrast, the more these three elements are disassociated, the less balanced the mind becomes. Moderation and self-control deteriorate. Conflict between the three elements grows leading to their mutual degradation. Consequently, nothing gets settled or decided. The mind becomes restive indulging in distractive thoughts and sinister designs. You become perturbed easily and invent excuses to justify your actions. Even though the intellect knows that responsibilities must be addressed and tasks performed, there is little motivation because you "can't get in the mood." Consequently, you are not physically up to the task.

"I know I have to get this done, but this-and-that is worrying me. How can I somehow get out of doing this?" Conniving and scheming like this indicates the width of the gap between the three elements. It is a major source of stress and a sign of a person's weakening character. The person starts to find excuses, voice complaints, and show resentment. Moreover, he or she begins to lose their sense of humility. They start blaming others when things go wrong. This is why people are neither able to make a firm decision nor are they able to just let go and give up. They cannot trust in others nor rely on themselves. Once these patterns become set in habit they become part of the person's character.

A person loses his or her dignity when desires take priority over any sense of shame or remorse. The balance between the three elements is so important that it even determines to what degree we perceive others as fellow human beings. In the enthusiasm to promote today's modern economic rationalism the significance and dignity of man have been disregarded. Ambition and craving have taken precedence constricting the relationship between the three elements. When the relationship between intellect, intent, and feelings is interrupted even for a moment, a person can instantaneously fly into a rage and start a commotion. In this state a person's tolerance gets stretched to the point where they helplessly lose all composure.

This kind of reckless behavior caused by the alienation of the three elements is a form of instinct, the primordial instinct to survive against a natural enemy in an endless struggle of the strong over the weak. It is karmic hindrance. Just the fact of being alive is itself one of life's mysterious phenomenon. Unmistakable, too, is the fact that the idea of a self is centered deep in consciousness. We must not forget this. This deep-seated idea of an ego is a kind of karmic hindrance that can take the form of man's cruelty and savagery. It arises from a basic "me first" instinct.

To practice the Buddha Way is to awaken to the True Self and resolve karmic hindrance, that is, to eliminate the habit of the three elements disuniting. There are expressions distinct to Zen, such as, "mind and body are one," "thoroughly penetrate," "become one," "liberation," "Enlightenment"; "forget the self," and so on. They all mean to eliminate this habit of the ego and to realize one's original nature. This is where the three elements have disappeared individually to fuse into one whole. When they have totally merged into one without any distinction among them, there is a tacit acknowledgement that the source of the three elements — mind and body — has fallen away. This is what Enlightenment is.

The mind that manifests Enlightenment is unobstructed by boundaries. There is no distinction of race, gender, past, or age. All distracting thoughts of profit and loss are transcended. Here one quite naturally acts in accord with the Way and the Buddha Dharma. A person does everything in his or her power to do their best. This is the form and substance of the wisdom realized by the ancient Buddhas and Masters. This is truly the wisdom of Prajna.

The only way to awaken to this is through the Zazen practice of *Shikantaza*—solely and single-mindedly sitting where even the sitting itself is forgotten. For the sake of our Zazen practice we throw away worldly thinking and vigorously foster "the Way-seeking

Mind." If we leave ourselves to the workings of the self-centered mind, we easily succumb to worldly-mindedness. As a consequence, the outcome is overindulgence, which denies us true tranquility of mind. What determines our future is our actions right here and now. What is important is to always distinguish between good and evil in the motives of our behavior, to perform selfless and nameless acts of kindness unbeknown to others, and to conduct ourselves in a way that does not contradict moral principles and good faith.

**The Mind of Non-Discrimination**

A baby has no desires, impure thoughts, or prejudices. He or she is egoless, uncontrived, and without cares of any kind. A baby is a pure and spontaneous creation of nature. Anyone would wish to have the pure mind of a baby. Therefore, the aim of religion is toward a pure mind such as this.

Originally, a baby's existence is totally spontaneous and without order, totally without the three elements of intellect, intent, and feelings. The five sense organs––eyes, ears, nose, tongue, and body––are the tools for "seeing, hearing, perceiving, and knowing"[12]. A baby is endowed with the five senses, but because the operation of each of the senses is not yet clearly distinguishable, they do not function together in a unified or systemic way. Consequently, a baby has no sense of self, no sense of being human, no sense of being alive, and no sense of being. To be sure, a baby's world is an undefiled world free of discrimination, but it would be impossible for us to live and conduct ourselves in such a world.

What I am trying to point out here is that Zen does not claim we should return to our infancy, but it does emphasize a particular and unique quality called the "mind of non-discrimination." This is the adult mind functioning soundly and healthily, without defilement or attachment. In other words, Zen is getting rid of the ego and self-centered thinking, and returning to one's original nature that is embodied in the ideal of the infant's mind of non-discrimination. The means of returning to one's original nature is Shikantaza.

It is no ordinary task for an adult, a self-respecting member of society who esteems decency, to return to the infant's mind of non-

___
12  Jap., *kenmon kakuchi.*

discrimination. It means awakening to a world, or a reality, before such things as self-consciousness, intellect, and thought arise. Here the notion of being human is no longer relevant; it is beyond the distinction of life and death. Therefore, if you want to awaken for yourself to what is called "the great matter" of Enlightenment, then first you must die "the great death." It means to make a fresh start by dying one time, in other words, forgetting the ego. You should understand both how difficult and how important this matter of Enlightenment is. It means to get to the very bottom of the matter.

Achieving this is the distinct trademark of Zen. Really throwing everything away to the extent necessary is no easy matter. This is what is called *shugyo*, the Japanese word meaning "religious practice." It means to commit yourself wholeheartedly and to endeavor undeterred by difficulties or suffering. This is the attitude needed for practicing Zen and for attaining the Buddha Way.

People commonly think that "mind" refers to words and ideas forming and manifesting as conceptualization. Although this is without a doubt an aspect of mind, everything that arises in consciousness is virtual in nature. *Virtual* means whatever arises in consciousness is no more than delusion, fantasy, and false perception. The original mind is formless. Since it manifests before discrimination, it precedes even consciousness. This is the mind of non-discrimination. When you have mastered the truth of the non-substantiality of things, all delusion, fantasy, and false perceptions disappear. This is the distinction between awakening and not awakening and the difference between delusion and Enlightenment.

Then, why does a baby, utterly pure and originally free of discrimination, become separated from this world of non-discrimination to create a world of bewilderment and conflict known as "the six realms of transmigration"[13], that is, the world of ordinary human beings? This is what is known as a person's karma. As a person learns to speak and to amass conceptual ideas, thought processes and sentiments naturally become more complex. Civilization and culture are shaped by the human ability to manage conceptual ideas and to deal with intellectual growth and development. Undoubtedly, the

---

13 The six realms of transmigration: heaven, humans, hell, hungry ghosts, brutes, and asuras.

more ably people can intellectually and thoroughly resolve whatever problems that confront them, the more society evolves and grows. This kind of ability and effort is most important.

However, the fact that such a capability can also cloud and corrupt the mind is problematic. It can incite social problems as well as instigate international dilemmas. This is because the desire for gratification and the need for self-assertion grow without being aware of it. This leads to a mentality that excels in self-justification and is quick to deceive and undermine others.

The stronger such things as self-consciousness, conception, and ideas become, the more obstinate the ego becomes and the more egotistical views grow. We should earnestly and carefully reflect on the dangers of how easily problems grow out of self-centered delusions, fantasies, and false perceptions.

Talented and gifted international leaders attempt to build up our already unimaginably destructive arsenal of arms without giving the slightest consideration regarding steps toward eliminating them. At the same time, when elementary school students are asked the simple question if people or countries should possess such weapons, the outcome is clear and simple. Young children respond that anything so dangerous, whose only purpose is for killing, should be thrown away. The underlying theme of Zen is to investigate the difference between these two ways the world is viewed and to establish their boundaries. This means establishing what we as humans consider to be the real nature of Truth.

It is due to the ego that we err. Therefore we must cultivate the practice of throwing away the ego and egotistic views. The Dharma gates of the Great Vehicle that Shakyamuni Buddha expounded are the ways for everyone to realize great peace of mind by throwing away the self. World peace is achieved when peace of mind is realized. The most powerful kind of collective security is to make peace in your own heart, to cherish mutual trust, and to live in harmony. It is absolutely necessary for people to cultivate themselves.

I have gotten completely off the subject. Let's return to the Heart Sutra.

**Sutra**

The Chinese character for sutra is pronounced "kyo" or "gyo" and refers to the lengthwise thread, or warp, of a piece of cloth. The warp threads must be uniform because if they snap, the fabric will buckle. From this meaning, the word *sutra* has assumed the meaning "ordinary," "unchanging," "truth," and "law." For example, the Chinese classic texts in the famous collection "The Four Books and Five Classics"[14] were referred to as sutras because the various teachings of sages and holy people were regarded as sutras. In other words, an important teaching was a sutra, and a collection of sutras was referred to as a sacred book.

Simply speaking, The Heart of the Perfection of Transcendent Wisdom is a sutra that expounds the essence of the Great Dharma. You should understand that it is a sacred scripture expounding the essential path leading to true liberation. In other words, it is a scripture expounding the path to true freedom by wholeheartedly devoting oneself to giving up the ego.

What is important is Genjo Sanzo's painstaking devotion to communicate the pure and unadulterated mind of Shakyamuni. It was Genjo's earnest request for us to endeavor in genuine practice of the Way without the fear of uncertainty. It was his wish that we realize the truth of the teaching for ourselves.

Our Zazen practice is to realize that The Heart of the Perfection of Transcendent Wisdom is the world of things just as they are. It is to actualize The Heart Of The Perfection Of Transcendent Wisdom simply as it is. There is no truth surpassing this. Therefore, one chants simply and directly, sound-for-sound:

*the-heart-of-the-per-fec-tion-of-tran-scen-dent-wis-dom.*

When chanting like this, if you are utterly absorbed in just that, the chanting becomes direct and clear. In short, becoming just the chanting itself there is 'no self,' and there are no self-centered ideas. It is in circumstances like this that you are able to awaken and resolve this great matter. When you awaken to this, it is the rebirth of the

---

14  Jap., *Shisho Gokyo.*

ancient master Yoka Daishi[15] ; it is the second coming of Osatsu[16]. This is the state of seeing directly into one's own nature and becoming Buddha. The Heart Sutra shows the way to personally experience the substance of this venerated teaching.

We are now approaching the main text of the sutra. Depending on how it is viewed, it can be divided into either three or five sections. The renowned teacher Kukai[17] divided it into five parts. However, in Zazen practice care should be taken not analyze too much. The world of Zen is beyond comparison. When you become one with things, the self drops off naturally and your original form manifests directly. This is why everything is settled and finished with Tenryu's holding up a finger, by Tozan's "three pounds of flax," Joshu's "mu"[18], and by the full circle drawn in the single brush stroke.

Now we are ready to begin the sutra.

---

15  Revered disciple of the sixth Chinese Zen patriarch.
16  Spirited and able laywoman disciple of Hakuin.
17  Japanese monk and founder of the Shingon sect of Buddhism in Japan.
18  Tenryu, Tozan, and Joshu are famous Chinese Zen masters of the 8th and 9th centuries.

# KANJIZAI BOSATSU...

### *"The bodhisattva Kannon..."*

The Heart Sutra begins with the bodhisattva Kannon expounding the teaching. For some people the teaching becomes easier to understand when they know who is speaking. For example, when we know that the bodhisattva Kannon is going to talk, it becomes clear that the essence of the Buddha Dharma is about to be revealed.

Here I'd like to make a remark about the meaning of *Kanjizai*, the name of the bodhisattva Kannon used in the Heart Sutra. This is a very important point in regard to Zazen practice and self-inquiry. If anyone finds what I am about to say insightful or applicably useful in their own practice, it will serve the Dharma all the more.

The kanji for *kan*, the first character of the word *Kan-ji-zai*, means "to observe." Seeing or observing is the condition where mountains and rivers and all of the great, wide earth appear when the eyes are opened. Although this is only natural, there is something very crucial here. It is that you know, or are aware, that you are seeing something. But even before becoming conscious of what you see, the fact is that the object is already reflected in the eye. Because the object is directly and instantly reflected in the eye, there is no time, or space, or gap for anything to intervene. The object appears instantaneously when the eye opens. In the wholeness of this activity of seeing there is no space for the slightest gap to occur. This state or condition before becoming conscious is where we must turn our attention. Since the reality of the eye seeing or the ear hearing precedes being conscious of it, its reality has nothing to do with consciousness or conception. This is an extremely important point.

When seeing, what is reflected in the eye is outside the world of conception and discrimination. What is seen in reality is not "a flower"; it is not "red", and it is not "pretty." What is reflected in the eye is originally pure and unblemished. Our six senses[19] truly do function and serve us well. At a glance, we know a flower from a human being and a parent from a child; we can tell the difference between a cow and a dog when hearing an animal cry out; and, we know if water is hot or cold the moment we touch it. This faculty of clear, direct and straightforward function is the wisdom of non-discrimination.

In this way, the eyes, ears, and other senses always function freely according to circumstances. This is called "observing without restriction," and is precisely the meaning of the Chinese characters for *Kanjizai*.

The ear hears, but before a person becomes conscious of what is heard, the ear has already picked up the sound. The sound is finished and past by the time it is perceived. This is the true state of the operation of all of our senses. That is to say, this reality — our existence — always manifests straight and direct without restriction or delusion. It is entirely irrespective of such things as consciousness, intellect, conception, words, or means of any kind. Our six senses operate thusly, and the entire universe functions accordingly. The practice of the Buddha Way is to wake up to this reality for ourselves.

This is the original and indestructible law of the cosmos. This is The Great Perfection of Transcendent Wisdom. The practice of the Buddha Way and the investigation into our Zen practice is to awaken to this pure and unadulterated natural law of the universe.

However, unless you have removed the gap between mind and body, it is not like this. You reside in the world of conception. It is like a shadow or dream of something that no longer exists — something created after the fact. The idea of seeing or hearing something takes shape from an event is already completed and finished, and is held in consciousness in the form of information. It is delusion, a fantasy,

---

19 Seeing, hearing, smelling, tasting, touching, and mental functions.

a false perception. It is something whose nature is virtual. It is what is called ignorance and false awareness. Everyone dwelling in the mundane world is deceived in this way. Those who cannot easily realize this Buddha refers to as sentient beings.

This is the reason we squander our lives and waste our existence meaninglessly. This is the ultimate opportunity being wasted. People are painfully weary of their confusion and strife. If you truly and earnestly reflect upon yourself and consider the possibility of profoundly altering your life, in an instant you can become acutely aware of the fleeting nature of time and the law of impermanence. Then it is possible to awaken "the Way-seeking Mind."

Dogen said, "The Way-seeking Mind clearly understands impermanence." If the Way-seeking Mind springs earnestly from the bottom of your heart, then you've really found it. It feels like the warm sun shining on the frozen earth. This is the time when the need for the Heart Sutra is greatest.

A bodhisattva is a true person of the Way. It is a person without delusion, fantasy, false perception, or ignorance. The bodhisattva Kannon is our own true selves, pure and undefiled. It is original, unrestricted freedom.

## *GYOJIN HANNYA HARAMITTA...*

### "Profoundly practicing Prajna Paramita..."

"Profoundly practicing" means doing a thing exhaustively, really getting to the bottom of the matter. It is Buddhist practice, casting aside both mind and body, and endeavoring day and night. Shinran, the founder of the True Pure Land School of Buddhism in Japan, encouraged his followers to chant the *Nenbutsu*[20] exhaustively, never forgetting it even while eating or lying down. This is an example of profoundly practicing.

To do Zazen is to do it exhaustively. When breathing, do it exhaustively. When studying, devote yourself with undivided attention and study exclusively. When preparing a meal, cleaning up, or taking a walk, do each thing devotedly without allowing miscellaneous

---

20 Repeating the name of Amida Buddha.

thoughts to intervene in what you are doing. Forgetting any notion of self, be devoted to the present moment we call 'now.' This is the meaning of "Profoundly practicing Prajna Paramita."

The question of what you should do 'now,' right this very moment, cannot be explained in a couple of words since each person's situation and circumstances differ. However, what can be said for everyone is that whatever you do should be done wholeheartedly and with single-minded devotion. Then it becomes the living and dynamic practice of the Buddha Way.

When one first takes up Zen practice, the mind does not settle down eaasily. The scattered mind and its habitual thinking constantly confuse and agitate the ordinary mind. This is true even when earnestly trying to concentrate on Zazen, or when focusing on one's breathing, or when trying to be absorbed in a simple daily activity such as walking.

Since we have no idea how to do Zazen at first, , our efforts are sloppy and haphazard. We are tortured by delusion, fantasy, and false perceptions. It makes us realize how stubborn and persistent the habit of distracted thinking is. In our habitual and usual way of thinking, thoughts line up together one after another, forming an unrelenting stream of fantasy and delusion. However, there is no need to become discouraged by this because it is just another temporary condition that will eventually pass. If you give up at times like this, nothing will be gained. But sustained by the Way-seeking Mind and strengthened by head-on determination, you must simply continue to fight to the end. Without fail, you can overcome the habit of being constantly distracted by thinking. This is because no matter how entrenched this habit may seem to be, it is fundamentally non-substantial in nature. Furthermore, since your cherish aim is awakening to the non-substantial nature of the universe, the distracted mind can without fail be subdued.

In any case, the important thing is to simply sit wholeheartedly and single-mindedly. If you devote your heart and soul to doing just one thing, you will naturally expend less time and energy on other useless mental activity. For example, suppose you are going to repair a ruptured water pipe. At first, you are bothered by curious onlookers gathering around. But because you have to make every possible effort to control the flooding water, you forget about the onlookers before you realize it. The more settled the mind becomes and the more absorbed you become in your work, the lighter both mind and body become. Wasted effort diminishes, and work goes more smoothly. Work efficiency optimizes when you really devote yourself single-mindedly to just the work itself.

It doesn't matter whether you are doing Zazen, breathing, or working. They are all the same. The more immersed you are in doing something, the less distracted you are by useless mental activity. With undivided attention just inhale and exhale. It is this very simple act of doing just that one thing, exhaustively and completely doing just that. At first you have to make an enormous effort to try to hold onto the breathing and to keep it right before you. It is a battle against idle thoughts and worldly desires. However, after a while of continually persevering with painstaking tenacity, even ideas of holding on and letting go start to subside. Then, without even making an effort to hold on to the breathing, the breathing no longer abandons or eludes you. You begin to see that from the beginning it has always been there right in front of you.

This is what you come to realize and become aware of. What you wake up to is known by many names: "the present moment," "just the thing itself," and "truth." It is called "thoughtless thought," "no mind," "a single thought cut off from before and after," "emptiness," and "the void." When the present moment is clarified, you see that thought and other mental activity are already finished and past by the time you become conscious of it. You gain the ability to ignore idle and miscellaneous thought. Little by little you gain the ability to just see and to just hear without the intervention of thought.

From this point on, you clearly see where the focus of Zen practice is and your practice instantly becomes easier. But until you do come to realize this, you will invariably get caught up in arising thoughts and be deluded in fantasy. You are then helpless and unable to escape from the habitually scattered mind. The best way to completely penetrate this matter is to ignore arising thoughts, leaving them as they are without dealing with them. However, if you can't see or understand this vital point, there is not a thing you can do. It is truly a shame when you cannot see where to make your effort.

Once you have the present moment in your grasp, both mind and body become lighter and everything appears so fresh you'd think your eyesight had sharpened. This shows how much the cluttered mind has started to settle down. What you should do now is to keep and preserve the present moment. This kind of effort is called expedient means. It means endeavoring single-mindedly to maintain the present moment and to break away from the habit of getting caught up in thought. In other words, to forget 'self and other,' you just become the present moment.

Let me explain a little more about expedient means. Expedient means to completely forget yourself and become utterly absorbed in what you are doing, giving your uninterrupted and undivided attention to the single task at hand. It is to breathe each breath meticulously with single-minded devotion. First, be aware of the start of inhaling. Then, make sure you stay with this one breath while inhaling. Finally, positively verify that this one inhale has ended. In other words, don't wander away from the breathing even for an instant.

Practicing like this will get rid of the habit of the mind becoming scattered. It is the most direct way to bring back the undivided oneness of body and mind. If you would merely continue to make effort in this way, the habit of ceaseless conceptual thought will naturally fall away. The habit of linking or stringing together thoughts, along with all concerns and entanglements, will naturally diminish and fall away.

In the practice of the Buddha Way there is no need to do anything special. From the time you get up in the morning until you go to sleep at night endeavor to have your feet on the ground at all times. Endeavor to keep miscellaneous thoughts from intervening, and strive untiringly to become one with whatever it is you are doing.

Zazen is revered because it is the path to eternal liberation attained by profoundly awakening to Supreme Enlightenment. "Personally reaching up for Enlightenment while reaching out to save of all sentient beings" is our guiding principle as we strive to forget the self completely and become one with the present moment. In other words, this is the essence of "Profoundly practicing Prajna Paramita." The teaching of the Heart Sutra urges us to exert ourselves in this way. The practice of the Buddha Way is directly transmitted from Shakyamuni Buddha. There is no room for doubt about this.

Next I will explain the outcome of devotedly endeavoring in this way.

# JISHO KEN GO ON KAI KU
# DO ISSAI KU YAKU...

*"When he clearly realized the five skandhas are completely empty, he was delivered from all suffering and pain..."*

Here the word *when* refers to this moment in time. It points to what is referred to as 'now,' the present moment. Truly, this awakening to reality is inevitable and a matter of course. It is not something encountered by coincidence or luck. *Clearly realized* means he penetrated to the absolute bottom of the matter; in other words, he "dropped off mind and body." The *five skandhas* are also called the "five aggregates" and refer to the collection of five kinds of causal factors, namely, form, sensation, conception, intent, and awareness. *Completely empty* means "non-substantial," "without any permanent form." It is the free and unrestricted ability to become anything in accordance with causal factors. Against the background of non-substantiality and unrestricted freedom, things are born, mature, decline, and end due to cause and effect

When you put food in your mouth, you taste it. However, it is impossible to extract the taste. This is because taste has no substantiality or true nature. As soon as the food passes down the throat, the cause and effect relationship is completed. Because it has no true form, nothing remains, and whatever the taste may have been completely disappears. Therefore, the next taste to appear materializes freely and unrestricted according to cause and effect.

The reason it works in this way is that it exists while at the same time having no substance or true nature of its own. Then, what is taste?It is both a sense and an illusion. Although there is nothing, things appear according to circumstances, or causal factors. Therefore things arise and pass straightforwardly and without bias, conflict, or disorder. This is the meaning of "...the five skandhas are completely empty."

The mind functions in the same way. The first person to discover this reality was Shakyamuni Buddha. He was the first person to realize the truth of complete emptiness. In other words, he demonstrated that the true form of all suffering and pain is utterly non-substantial in nature. When one reaches this realm of great peace and contentment, there is no realm more supreme.

Let's take a closer look. The five skandhas are form, sensation, conception, intention, and awareness. *Skandha* means "store house" or "supply." It is an aggregate, or a collection of things. *Form* is things and people. Sensation, conception, intention, and awareness are processes or workings of the mind. Our bodies are endowed with the six sense organs: eyes, ears, nose, tongue, body, and mind. These sense organs perceive objects which allows us to "see, hear, perceive, and know." Due to the five skandhas our physical bodies appear in its present form, but in essence our bodies have no true form. We function day in and day out, with all of our activities depending on the operation of the five skandhas.

When someone pinches you, it hurts. This hurt is the same as the sense of taste or the senses of seeing and hearing. The pain has no true form or substantiality of its own. What you see, hear, or feel cannot be grasped or fastened down in any way. Due to the nature of cause and effect, when the causes disappear, the pain disappears. In the case of seeing or hearing, no trace whatsoever remains in the eyes or ears. Nothing remains from whatever has just been seen or heard. So our eyes, ears, and bodies always function freely without restriction. Moreover, the senses do not undergo change or alteration of any kind due to what they see, hear, and so on. Furthermore, if the causal link once again appears and you are pinched again, the pain can arise over again at any time.

The point is that it is very important to realize that everything occurs due to cause and effect and that in the present moment things appear only provisionally in their present form. It is important to awaken to this fact for yourself. This is the purpose of Zen practice.

It is the same for building a house or for making a kimono. Construction begins with lumber. The lumber is combined with various other building materials, and the house is completed. A kimono starts with weaving the cloth one thread at a time. Whether talking about houses or clothes, or discussing lumber or thread, things themselves have no true form of their own. Therefore things can be made freely in any shape and size, and they can extinguish or be destroyed at any time. This is both universal law and the true form of reality. This is the import of "…the five skandhas are completely empty."

When you have completely penetrated Zazen practice, this state of reality will clarify itself for you. The moment you clarify the reality of 'no true form,' the four basic sufferings, the three poisons[21], and all troubles that plagued you will instantaneously melt away. This is the essence of the verse of the Heart Sutra that says, "When you clearly realize the five skandhas are completely empty, you are delivered from all suffering and pain."

At the time of birth when we give out our first cry, we are already furnished with our six senses. This is our physical body. Since this physical body of ours with its collection of various functions originated through causal factors provided through our parents, it has no true or concrete form. Furthermore, when these causal conditions are exhausted or have run their course, this body will return to its natural origin. This is what is called emptiness. But since we don't realize this for ourselves, problems arise.

The fundamental source of our problems is self-consciousness. Sometime at an early age, before we even become aware of it, we become attached to the notion that this mind and body is ourselves. We think that this mind and body exist, even though it has no true or concrete form. Here we start to identify or distinguish between ourselves and others, and then we cannot get rid of the notion. At the moment we begin to perceive this body as ourselves, then, relatively,

---

21 Greed, anger, and ignorance.

the notion of 'other,' or 'others,' arises. Here is where egotistical views and the "self-other" dichotomy are established.

Due to this, mind and body separate. It is from this time on that the mind, like a flickering ghost, begins to wonder and waver pointlessly. In other words, the mind falls into the habit of racing about throughout the realm of consciousness ceaselessly wondering around lost in an expanse of conception and thought. The mind falls into the habit of spontaneously raising notions of 'self and other,' viewing things relatively, and weighing the pros and cons of things. This is why you become anxious over external circumstances, why people and things trouble you, and why things you see and hear agitate you. The mind haunts us endlessly with thoughts of choosing between this and that, of conflicts between gain and loss, and of quibbling over likes and dislikes.

At this stage, if passion, resentment, or discontent also well up, intense emotion, suspicion, and fear are generated. Eventually, this whole concoction spills over into turmoil and argument. Ultimately conflict and struggle ensue. No matter how calm a person's outward appearance may seem, people have always had to struggle because strife and conflict remain unmanageable by means of reason or good intentions. The three poisons and the four basic sufferings are the source of tremendous delusion. The source of delusion is the gap created between mind and body. When mind and body return to their original oneness, we become empty and free and are always intimately one with cause and effect. This is what penetrating this matter is about. It means peace and contentment.

It took Shakyamuni Buddha over six years of strenuous religious austerities to overcome his suffering. He relentlessly punished his mind and body to their extremes. However, he came to see that all his efforts had been mistaken. He realized that what he had to do was to actually endeavor in a way not using mind or body, in other words, he had to leave everything just as it is. This is Zazen. What happens when it isn't necessary to endure anything? The problem was that he was searching of something.

Anyone can hold their bodies motionless, but it is very difficult at first to hold the mind still. It was the same for Shakyamuni. Since he was being tormented by a deluge of idle thoughts and worldly desires, he resolved to clarify the true character of his various thoughts. The only way for him to resolve this was to clarify their origin. How do you investigate their origin or source? The only way is to pay close attention to the present moment as it arises and as it passes. There is no other way. This is what Shakyamuni realized by focusing on the present moment and penetrating closer and closer to its source. To say it in another way, by continually brushing aside idle thoughts and worldly desires he closed in on the source where mind arises. He found that the best approach for doing this was Zazen. At the end of six years he became one with Zazen and finally reached the source where everything was clarified.

About 2600 years ago on December 8 at dawn Shakyamuni glimpsed the morning star through the haze while sitting on a rock in the forest. Shakyamuni and the morning star became one; rather, before there was any time for delusion to arise, there was absolutely nothing — no self and no other — and he became one with what he saw. Here he realized that everything was empty. He profoundly awakened proclaiming:

> *All beings, sentient and insentient, and myself together attain the Way. Mountains, rivers, the grasses, and trees altogether realize Buddha.*

This is the essence of the line in the Heart Sutra, "...clearly realized the five skandhas are completely empty, he was delivered from all suffering and pain."

How truly significant Shakyamuni Buddha's realization of this great matter was in regard to the redemption of all of humankind! It was the moment that humankind first attained the path to complete and genuine salvation. This is why he is venerated as "The Great Sage Shakyamuni Buddha." The physical and mental discipline he acquired through strenuous religious practice was highly refined. His sensory perception and observational powers were delicately and thoroughly polished. He was in a state far beyond normal.

The six senses and their corresponding sense objects are the means by which pain arises. This is true for all bodily sensation. All that we see, hear, perceive, and know is due to the operation of the six senses. The senses simply function moment by moment according to causal factors. This means things have no true form. Things arise spontaneously and unconditionally, and they are clearly independent of human thought. This is Truth. This is the Dharma.

However, we get drawn in, or become captivated, by what we see and hear. This sets into motion various thoughts and illusions. This is the ordinary state of our lives and how our minds habitually work. In other words, we begin to raise various thoughts and notions one after another. This is called worldly thought. Shakyamuni discovered that the continual arising of mundane thinking develops from a composite of the four mental skandhas of sensation, perception, intent, and awareness.

This kind of observation and realization could only have been accomplished by someone like Shakyamuni. He clarified the source of delusion, something utterly inexplicable by means of reasoning or science, and he elucidated the means to resolve human suffering. As may be expected, it had to be someone like Shakyamuni Buddha, the World-Honored One. We stand in veneration to his devotion and exhaustiveness in his search of the True Way.

It is astounding that he was able to pinpoint the source of continuously arising thoughts and mental phenomena. It is said that these phenomena arise at a rate of more than 1000 each second. In other words, in the time it takes to snap one's fingers more than 900 thoughts arise and pass.

When a man sees a woman, at the instant he is conscious of the woman. Ideas of beauty and ugliness, of yearning, and a multitude of other feelings are set in motion. Notions and awareness of 'space and time' and 'past and future' are triggered simultaneously. Instantly, the entire mind swiftly and furiously becomes utterly engulfed in conception, delusion, and fantasy. From the results of Shakyamuni's observations, it was realized that in the interval it takes to blink the eye about 900 such mental events occur. Here we can see the ferocity of the habit that shackles us and makes us slaves to thought and conceptualization.

It is said that a blink of the eye takes as little as 1/50 of a second. A snap of the fingers lasts about the same amount of time. Shakyamuni's keen insight on the remarkable speed that thoughts arise was no simple task. It could only have been perceived as a result of great risk and at disregard for personal life. "When he clearly realized the five skandhas are completely empty, he was delivered from all suffering and pain" means to penetrate, realize, and personally experience this great matter.The Heart Sutra is the essence of the Buddha's teaching and his personal message of awakening. It is truly concise and flawless.

Now it is time for Buddha to turn the Great Wheel of the Dharma. Focusing on his ten closest disciples, he begins to convey the Dharma's message to others. In particular, he turns his eyes to Sariputra.

# SHARISHI...

### *"Sariputra!..."*

Shakyamuni compellingly calls Sariputra telling him to listen
well. He is expecting Sariputra's complete attention. The path of
Buddha is the unsurpassed Great Way. If you really forget the ego,
everything will be resolved. Shakyamuni admonishes Sariputra to
investigate the Way more and more diligently pointing out what is
clearly lacking in his practice of penetrating the present moment.

Now Buddha's ten closest disciples along with the entire
community of followers are all inspired to practice the Way more
diligently. "If you have not yet awakened to your true nature as I
have taught, then you are not really free from suffering," Shakyamuni
expounds the Dharma impressing the teaching deeply upon each
person while, at the same time, checking their grasp of it.

The energy and spirit of the entire Heart Sutra is in itself the
compassion of Shakyamuni Buddha. Because his ten closest disciples
were already endowed with a certain degree of clear-sightedness, he
was able to remove any tinge or stain of enlightenment that hindered
them and was able to lead them to Great Enlightenment.

Buddha calls Sariputra two times in this short sutra. This indicates
the high expectations Buddha had for him. Moreover, any use of
metaphors or figurative speech in the Heart Sutra was avoided. This
is because those he was preaching to were his earnest followers

who needed only the direct teaching of the Dharma along with a strengthened resolve to seek the Way.

Shakyamuni Buddha is giving an impassioned sermon on the precious Dharma. This impassioned sermon is like a lion's roar by the king of beasts, expounding the all-pervading Dharma in order to rescue all beings without leaving anyone behind.

### *SHIKI FU I KU KU FU I SHIKI SHIKI SOKU ZE KU KU SOKU ZE SHIKI JU SO GYO SHIKI YAKU BU NYOZE...*

*"Form is not different than emptiness; emptiness is not different than form. That which is form is empty; that which is emptiness is form. This is also true for sensation, perception, intention, and awareness...."*

Here the sutra clarifies in detail the relationship between form and emptiness to demonstrate the completeness and profundity of the Dharma.

*Form* is people and things. That is, it is form, it is differentiation, and it is the myriad causal factors. It is the entire universe itself. Moreover, it encompasses all causality in terms of both time and space. This is what is called non-substantiality.

Everything in the universe undergoes constant change. A newborn child has the face of an infant. Gradually its gender becomes clear, and it takes on the appearance of a little boy or girl. Before we know it, spring becomes summer, and summer turns into fall, all due to an entangling web of infinite circumstances and causal factors throughout the entire universe. This is the form of the present moment, which is ever-changing. The present moment certainly exists, while at the same time, it does not. It is because of this constant change that our lives take form. It is what life itself is, and, at the same time, it is the true form of all things.

This is what is called cause and effect, or the law of causality, because all things arise due to causal factors and circumstances. It is proof that things have no self-nature or substantiality of their own. It is the demonstration of emptiness. Since there is nothing that is exclusive of the fact that all form is empty, there is no mistake in thinking that the working of emptiness, too, is form. Simply stated, this means that

> "...form is not different than emptiness; emptiness is not different than form. That which is form is empty, that which is emptiness is form. This is also true for sensation, perception, intention, and awareness."

In regard to the four skandhas of sensation, perception, intent, and awareness, each is dependent on the causal factors of just a particular moment in time. Each one arises and functions separately. The operation of each of the skandhas occurs and concludes by itself. None of them are either connected or work in sequence. Each is one instance of causality and its form is empty. You should come to understand that originally all things are cut off from before and after.

In other words, everything is none other than mind. Thinking as it is, thoughts as they are, sensation as it is, whatever arises at that particular moment is just what it is 'as it is' at that moment. Even if you look back to see it, there is nothing there.

In short, the point is that we become bewildered and confused because of our involvement with arising thoughts. If we get to the bottom of this matter, mind and body become one. When mind and body are one, there is no more attachment to thinking or looking back at the past. In short, penetrate to the source of this moment and master it.

# SHARISHI...

### *Sariputra, behold!*

The second time Buddha calls Sariputra's name is like a bolt of thunder. It is the same as being grabbed by both coat lapels. Buddha's dignified bearing and piercing eyes would make the devil himself quiver and beg for mercy. "If you don't throw away everything and investigate to the source of the matter, you will never awaken to the profound Dharma that I am about to expound."

This is heaping kindness upon kindness. It is enough to give you goose bumps.

### *ZE SHOHO KUSO FUSHO FUMETSU FUKU FUJO FUZO FUGEN...*

**"All dharmas are the form of emptiness. They are not born nor do they die, are neither sullied nor pure, nor do they increase or decrease..."**

*All dharmas* means the inherent working of all things. In other words, it is the functioning of water and fire, of the eyes and the tongue. It is the working of all creation. Because all things appear due to causality, their form is empty. Because the form of all things is empty, whatever may appear and however it may appear depends entirely on cause and effect. All things emerge from one and the same source. Therefore a person does not remain a person, a flower does not stay a flower, and life does not remain life. Life has no substantiality of its own. Due to causes and conditions, life appears. Once again, due to causes and conditions, there is death. Since death has no substantiality or true form of its own, it is due to causes and circumstances that we die. Without causes and circumstances there is no death.

Life is life. Within life itself there is no death. Life can be nothing other than life. It is completely life. Death is also the same. It is the spontaneous and natural working of the universe, in other words, the state of emptiness.

Things like 'birth and death' and 'pure and impure' appear because we raise ideas of 'before and after' and begin to make comparisons. These are the views of people who are attached to shape and form. They are descriptions. They are attachments to names and forms. In the working of cause and effect as it is, there are no such hindrances. It is due to delusion, fantasy, and false perception that we attach names and descriptions to things. The way to get rid of this habit is through the practice of the Buddha Way. By realizing the non-substantiality of what deludes us, we are awakened to the true form of emptiness.

In things as they are, there are no obstacles or hindrances. At all times, everything is completed and concluded as it is. Therefore, simply by leaving things as they are according to cause and effect you can get rid of this habit of being attached to names and forms. Endeavoring like this, the time will come without a doubt when you realize the true nature of emptiness. Then all obstacles will drop away. You will clearly come to understand the true nature of nothingness and of things simply as they are. You will live free and unconstrained. This is where the working of salvation is explained in detail. In essence, it is awakening to the world of things just, or simply, as they are: it is the realm of the thing itself.

For this reason it is necessary to get rid of the self, which is an obstacle to awakening. Doing this is the work of the teacher. It is the measure of his or her ability to guide the student to awakening to things just as they are by demonstrating the Dharma and removing the student's attachments.

The reality of the present moment is the form of emptiness. Therefore, how can things like 'birth and destruction' or 'purity and defilement' arise? This means you should immediately throw away all such views as 'birth and destruction,' 'purity and defilement,' and 'gain and loss'. Throw away all perspectives that depend on the ego and are grounded in consciousness. In this way the Heart Sutra explains that in the present moment such obstacles do not exist because "...they are not born nor do they die, are neither sullied nor pure, nor do they increase or decrease." They are empty of any true form of their own and simply appear according to causes and conditions.

In the next lines the Heart Sutra makes the same point, this time using nothingness rather than emptiness to dismantle and strip away the existence of obstacles.

# ZE KO KU CHU MU SHIKI MU JU SO GYO SHIKI MU GEN NI BI ZESSHIN NI MU SHIKI SHO KO MI SOKU HO MU GEN KAI NAI SHI MU I SHIKI KAI...

*"For this reason, in emptiness there is no form, nor is there sensation, perception, intention, or awareness. There are no eyes, ears, nose, tongue, body, or mind; and no form, sound, smell, taste, touch, or mental formations. There are no realms of sight, and so on, through to no realm of consciousness..."*

With "no form," "no eyes," "no sight," and so on, the sutra expounds the condition of nothingness[22]. The Heart Sutra dismantles and sweeps away the spheres of consciousness associated with the senses in order to demonstrate their being empty. First of all, the matter of emptiness is taken up. Next, the sutra discusses in length the relevance of names and forms based on the understanding that things such as mental operations and sensory functions have neither substance nor true nature of their own.

However, even if you get rid of words, names, and concepts, something that is hot is still hot, salt is still salty, and sugar is still sweet. These things are facts. They are the undeniable Dharma. In

---

22 Jap., *mu.*

these things, there is no ego or self to be found. This is the mind of non-discrimination and the wisdom of Prajna Paramita. In order to really realize this for yourself it is absolutely necessary to separate from names, forms, and concepts. When we start linking words and concepts one after another, we separate from truth and lose our original nature which is free from all concerns.

Throwing away everything means absolutely everything, including mental operations and sensory functions too. It means to throw away both mind and body. The Heart Sutra says, in other words, to throw away the self. To throw away the self means to forget the self. This is what the teaching of nothingness stresses. In other words, sensation, perception, intention, and awareness function freely of themselves, without relying on consciousness or on the ego. Simply give yourself up to the functioning of the eyes, ears, nose, tongue, body, and mind: just see, hear, smell, taste, touch, and think.

Suppose you are able to get that far in your practice. Through emptiness, nothingness, and leaving everything simply as it is, you are able to throw away absolutely everything. However, when you do throw everything away, there is absolutely nothing left to do. What do you do then? From the standpoint of the teaching, this is exactly where you should be. Having nowhere to turn and being utterly lost is exactly where you do absolutely nothing. Use neither mind nor body. Don't move, don't see, don't hear, don't think, don't live, don't die. Here you simply be the present moment. You just give everything over to cause and effect as it is. This is how the Heart Sutra prods the student of the Way to awakening by leading him or her to cut off the root of consciousness.

When Daito Kokushi[23] initially awakened, he asked numerous masters to check this attainment. None of them could find fault with his attainment, but Daito was somehow still dissatisfied. He still hadn't completely dropped off the ego. Later, as it turned out, he was able to meet Daio Kokushi. As soon as they met, Daito hastily began questioning Daio about the Dharma. Daio Kokushi interrupted Daito saying, "Let's have some tea first." But Daito replied, "Life and death are vital matters. Transience is swift. There is no time for tea." Daio simply told him, "You don't know what the Buddha Dharma is, do

---

23 National Teacher Daito: Rinzai Zen master of 14th century Japan.

you." With that brief reply Daio cast aside all of Daito's ideas about enlightenment, practice, and understanding. It was like Daio saying, "What could there be outside the Buddha Dharma? The Buddha Dharma is this very moment, isn't it? When drinking tea, just drink tea. Isn't that what the Buddha Dharma is?"

Afterward, when Daito penetrated his Zazen practice and awakened to the inner meaning of the present moment, Daio proclaimed that Daito was "the second coming of Unmon."[24]

Daito Kokushi's literary work, *Stories from Kaian*[25] is truly matchless. It is indeed a treasure book for the practitioner who has had an initial awakening experience, although it would be beyond the grasp of ordinary laypeople. The depth of understanding of both Unmon and Daito was unusually profound. Coincidentally, both masters suffered from leg disabilities. Unmon's older Dharma brother was Ganto. Unmon's master was the famous Chinese Zen master Seppo, and Seppo's master was Tokusan

Revered master Joshu lived during the same era. Joshu awakened at 18, and for the next 40 years he refined his enlightenment practicing under his teacher Nansen. When Joshu was 60, he set out on a pilgrimage that was devoted to continuing his practice by visiting famous masters of the time. He was without a doubt a master among masters. At the age of 80 he began to receive disciples, and in his lifetime he raised 20 excellent ones.

Gen'yo was a young trainee when he asked master Joshu, "I am new here. How should I practice the Way?" Joshu replied, "Have you eaten breakfast yet?" Gen'yo answered, "Yes, I have." "Then you've probably washed your bowls." With just this one remark, Gen'yo immediately understood the significance of the present moment. It was a significant insight for Gen'yo in his practice of the Buddha Way. He saw that Zen practice is to separate from all reasoning and to simply and solely do right now what should be done. Later on, he experienced Great Enlightenment becoming a teacher of all heaven and earth. It was Gen'yo who compiled the famous *Annals of Joshu.*

---

24  Unmon: famous Zen master of early 10th century China
25  Jap., *Kaian Kokugo*

The Heart Sutra states, "…in emptiness...no sensation, perception, intention, or awareness." I would like to elaborate on this. When a sensation is felt or experienced, there is only that. Perception, intention, and awareness come into play, but the time when each of these arises is different. They are not connected in any way. Each functions only at a particular time and finishes in itself. Here is where you find the substance of Zen and the vital force of the Buddha Dharma. This is what nothingness is. If you clarify this point, before and after will be cut off. You will awaken directly and everything will be settled.

Nothingness is leaving things as they are. It is not getting involved. If you leave things as they are, sensation, perception, and so on, don't link together or somehow become connected. This is the meaning of nothingness. It is the state of dropping off mind and body. When you really come to understand this, you realize the truth of non-substantiality that the true form of things is no form. When you really grasp this, mind and body drop off.

Then, how do you leave sensation alone and not become involved? Precisely right here is where you find the vital point of leaving things as they are. It is leaving the functions of seeing, hearing, perceiving, and knowing just as they are. Just see, just hear. Leave things as they are, pay them no mind, and don't deal with them. It means to ignore the workings of the eyes, ears, nose, tongue, body, and mind. In other words, it means to simply or just see, to simply hear, and so on.

Thought instantly comes into play when the skandhas of sensation, perception, intention, and awareness become active. This is what the mind does by nature, and left as it is there is no problem at all. But it is important to understand why our customary or habitual way of employing the four skandhas is mistaken.

Commonly speaking, sensation, perception, intention, and awareness begin to function when we erect a self and perceive something objectively that is outside or separate from ourselves. We intentionally take notice of something and begin dealing with it by comparing, judging, and probing. This is where the problem lies. At that instant the mind ground stirs making waves of disquiet and discord.

In short, even though the original functioning mind is formless, we intentionally erect a self and fall into delusion, fantasy, and false ideas. This is how the stream of sensation, perception, intention, and awareness operates. This is why we become anxious about things. It is because we create a self-other dichotomy. This is the source of conflict and discord. Because we want to have the upper hand, the evil mind begins to scheme, leading us into suffering, confusion, and strife. First, we must recognize this habit. In short, you should realize clearly that you see things through the ego which habitually becomes engaged in the stream of sensation, perception, intention, and awareness, which leads to confusion and strife. Because we don't realize this habit, it becomes our usual way of seeing things. Through the eyes of Buddha it is truly an upside down view of the world.

What happens is that you come up with some half-baked conclusions about things that even you yourself don't firmly believe in. Perhaps you stubbornly hold on to some notion knowing that it creates confusion around you or for some reason doesn't even sit quite right with you yourself. Such things occur because something is interfering or standing in the way. What is standing in the way is the self. It is the gap between 'mind and body' and the perception of 'self and others.' This is truly a vital matter.

We think, feel, and imagine. When these things are finished and over, nothing remains because things have no true, or real, form of their own. Therefore there is nothing to pursue or act on and no self who gets involved. Whatever the circumstances, everything is properly settled and in order. This is the meaning of "no sensation, perception, intention, or awareness." If you haven't awakened to the reality that mind and body are one, then sensation, perception, intention, and awareness only result in delusion, fantasy, and false perception.

What has just been talked about is also true for the next line.

# MU GEN NI BI ZESSHIN NI MU SHIKI SHO KO MI SOKU HO...

*"No eyes, ears, nose, tongue, body, or mind; no form,*
*sound, smell, taste, touch, or mental formations..."*

The six sense organs and the six sense objects make up our mind and body and its functions.Nothingness is the free and unrestricted use of all of the senses. It is independent of conditions, processes, or needs. Being free from the likes, dislikes, and preferences, all of these spectacular faculties simply function moment by moment. Each operation ends without anything remaining. Existing provisionally for the moment, things disappear at once when finished. This is how the six sense organs are able to function freely and unconditionally moment by moment. This crisp and concise yet unlimited activity which leaves no traces is known as liberation, or salvation. This is the meaning of nothingness. The Buddha Way is to realize the true nature of things, to untie the fetters binding you, and to freely enjoy the true form of emptiness. This is the substance of "No eyes, ears, nose, tongue, body, or mind; no form, sound, smell, taste, touch, or mental formations."

Mind itself has no true nature. In spite of this, its function is like a pilot dealing with all of the information available to it. Mind and Dharma become one when you know what the Way is, when you know who you yourself are, when you know the reality of cause and effect, and when you know that a mistake is a mistake.

It is important to understand that when the eye sees, the eye itself has no notion or idea that it is seeing. Also, when hearing, the ear itself doesn't know it is hearing. There are only the free and unrestricted functions of seeing, hearing, perceiving, and knowing. Without an ego, the six senses function freely just as they are. This is Nirvana. All of us are this natural, spontaneous, and unexcelled creation. The practice of the Buddha Way is to grasp this fact and attain great peace of mind. As long as the self exists, you will never be free from the nexus of sensation, perception, intention, and awareness that links you to confusion and strife. Because you have not awakened, evil thoughts and deceit prevent you from escaping transmigration in the six realms of ordinary existence.

In any case, you should just sit Zazen earnestly, forgetting the four aggregates, the six senses, and the six sense objects. If you penetrate to the bottom of this matter, before and after will be cut off and you will realize nothingness.

For the sake of brevity, the phrase "No realm of vision…through to no realm of consciousness" has been shortened. This makes the meaning a little difficult to understand without explaining in a little more detail.

The six sense organs along with their corresponding sense objects make up twelve, what are referred to as, "fields." Furthermore, each of the six senses has corresponding fields of consciousness. So more precisely speaking, there are six sense organs, six sense objects, and a consciousness for each of the six senses. This makes eighteen fields all together. Therefore, as it is written in the sutra, the line begins with "No realm of vision…" and implies passing through the next 16 fields similarly. Then it takes up the last and 18th field, the field of consciousness for mental formations. It explains that while the true nature of consciousness has no real form, it functions spontaneously and naturally in the moment. The sutra explains that in reality there is absolutely nothing at all. When truly seeing, there is nothing to see and no one who sees. This in essence is the main point. The Heart Sutra goes into detail elaborating on the nature of non-substantiality, but it all boils down to removing the gap and awakening to the truth that mind and body are one. This means penetrating to the bottom of this vital matter and forgetting the self.

Why did Shakyamuni Buddha, whose teaching is always so scrupulous and precise, leave this out of the Heart Sutra? It is because his 10 closest disciples had already mastered the Dharma to some degree. In urging his disciples to devote themselves, Shakyamuni was saying that the reason they haven't clearly grasped the teaching of non-substantiality is because they still recognize an ego self.

# MU MUMYO YAKU MU MUMYO JIN NAISHI MU RO SHI YAKU MU RO SHI JIN...

*"There is no ignorance, nor is there cessation of ignorance. There is no old age and death, and no cessation of old age and death..."*

Nothingness is another name for emptiness. It means "without form." Without an ego, there is no ignorance. If there is ego, there is delusion, fantasy, and false perception. These are the source of ignorance. As long as there is a self, you will not understand truth, and there will be no end to ignorance. In this way Buddha mercifully expounded the Dharma explaining, "There is no ignorance, nor is there cessation of ignorance."

Chopsticks are chopsticks. They are chopsticks through and through. Chopsticks have no self. Chopsticks are without ego. Zazen is Zazen. Zazen is without ego. If you can not agree or consent to this fact, then your ignorance is all the greater. It means you are still attached to the ego. If you really get to the bottom of something, there is just the thing itself. At that moment, things as they are show you their true nature.

Originally, for both Zazen and chopsticks there is no illumination or darkness; there is just Zazen, just chopsticks. In things just as they are there is no room for reasoning or interpretation. There is absolutely nothing extra, nothing other than the thing itself. When you penetrate Zazen, it will show you there is no self, no center. It will demonstrate the truth of non-substantiality. Zen practice is to realize this one great matter.

### *"There is no old age and death, and no cessation of old age and death..."*

Old age and death represent "the four basic sufferings" of birth, old age, sickness, and death. The four sufferings and the four kinds of birth in the six realms are all mind, and they are all the form and shape of delusion. Delusion manifests due to the gap between mind and body. This gap is created by the ego self. To thoroughly penetrate old age and death is to thoroughly penetrate the present moment. When this happens, you will realize there is no self in old age and death as they are, and you will be fully assured that if there is no self, then there is no old age and death. Birth, old age, sickness, and death are ordinary and common events of human life. They are never-ending. This is the meaning of "No old age and death, and no cessation of old age and death... ."

Because sensation, perception, intention, and awareness are part of human nature, they will never come to an end. Furthermore, the six senses do not exist, and they will never come to an end. All of these things do not exist and do not come to an end. This is the message that is communicated to you when you penetrate this matter and realize that body and mind are one.

Zen practice is not torturing your body doing ascetic practices. It is to simply practice, being one with the moment without looking elsewhere and without being distracted. Doing Zen practice in this way is the living Heart Sutra. Our entire daily lives are the Dharma—cooking, cleaning, or washing your face. Simply do it without looking or seeking elsewhere. Be one with the activity, and you will become intimate with the Dharma. This is awakening through cause and effect. The most important thing is to be truly intimate with each moment. To be intimate means to penetrate.

Shido Bunan, the early 17th century Japanese Zen master, said originally there is no such thing as "no form, sound, smell, taste, touch, or mental formations." He went on to say there is no such thing as "no realm of sight...through to no realm of consciousness." Bunan then continued on to say the same about "no ignorance and no cessation of ignorance." Finally, he sums up it all up saying that originally there is no such thing as "not existing." Bunan wrote:

> Nothingness is not something expressible in words. Once you forget even nothingness, then true nothingness manifests. To think about not thinking about something is itself thinking about it. Forget even about not thinking.

This verse is truly a concise, direct, and fascinating way of explaining nothingness.

# MU KU SHU METSU DO MU CHI YAKU MU TOKU I MU SHO TOKKO BO DAI SATTA E HAN NYA HA RA MITTA KO SHIN MU KE GE MU KE GE KO MU U KU FU ON RI ISSAI TEN DO MU SO KU GYO NEHAN...

*"There is no suffering, no cause or annihilation of suffering, and no path to liberation. There is no wisdom or attainment. Because there is no attainment, the Bodhisattvas depend on Prajna Paramita. The mind of Prajna Paramita is without hindrance. Without hindrance, there is no fear. Going far beyond all upside-down views and attaining Nirvana..."*

These lines are quite intriguing. They are a grand summarization of nothingness. In regard to the phrase, "no suffering, cause or cessation of suffering, and no path to liberation," Bunan says,

"In emptiness, there is no suffering, no cause of suffering, no annihilation of suffering, and no path to liberation."

He sweeps them all aside. When you multiply anything by zero, it becomes zero. Zazen is zero. Zero is the moment you utterly penetrate Zazen. Zero is Buddha. This is the essence of 'simply' — simply seeing, simply doing. It is "Mountains, rivers, the grasses, and trees all together realize Buddha." It is Shakyamuni Buddha.

When Buddha first began to turn the Wheel of the Dharma[26], he taught that as long as mind and body exist, human life is "suffering, causes and extinction of suffering, and the Way." He used this as a means to comfort those he was teaching, like giving candy to a crying child to make the youngster stop crying.

But Bunan responds to this teaching of Buddha saying, "I don't swallow it. Where can you find suffering or the cessation of suffering in this one breath I take now? In standing, walking, lying down, sitting, drinking tea or eating, or any other ordinary activity in our daily lives, where can you find anything defiled or impure? If you claim such things exist, bring them out this instant so we can see. Previously, you joyfully exclaimed, 'All beings, sentient and insentient, and myself together attain the Way.' Is that a lie now?"

Bunan brandishes the truth of original nothingness pressing Buddha for an answer.

In the beginning Buddha expounded the Four Noble Truths and the Eight-Fold Path. This was a famous sermon when he first turned the Wheel of the Dharma. At that time his teaching was presented from the standpoint of sentient beings suffering and bound by attachment. Everyone found the explanation of the origin of suffering understandable and gratefully accepted it. This shows there is a Dharma teaching aimed at children and a Dharma teaching for grownups. It is a way of adapting the teaching to the situation.

But here in the Heart Sutra Buddha denies what he previously says, proclaiming the opposite now by declaring that there is "no suffering, no cause of suffering...," and so on. Therefore, it is impossible to simply take his teaching at face value. The reason for Buddha's double-dealing here is to intervene a little for the sake of the Dharma in order not to confuse future generations of unenlightened people.

---

26 i.e., expound the teaching of the Buddha Dharma.

It is as if Bunan has stripped naked and exposed Buddha, and Buddha looks away smiling faintly in a way trying to convey, "That's why I say that originally this is not so. What I am saying here is precisely the reason why there is no suffering, no cause of suffering, and no extinction of suffering in the present moment."

The essence of the Eight Fold Path is to refine and temper one's Zen practice and to profoundly awaken to one's original nature. The path to achieving this is presented in the Heart Sutra where the underlying teaching is nothingness, which is the denial of the existence of suffering, its causes and cessation, and so forth. This is the quintessence and soul of Shakyamuni Buddha. It is the true and actual world transcending suffering, its causes and cessation, and the Eight Fold Path. When you penetrate the Way, this becomes clear. Said in another way, if you forget mind and body and live absolutely in the here and now, you will realize personally that the teaching of suffering and the cessation of suffering were merely expedient means.

If you think a strong will is the only thing needed to tackle Zen practice, you will find it very difficult to become single-mindedly absorbed in sitting Zazen. If there is some activity that you have a passion for or are good at, or if you participate in a competitive game of skill, then you become totally absorbed in what you are doing. You forget completely about sleep, food, or the cold. You could happily do it all day long without any problem. On the other hand, if you are doing something unpleasant or troublesome, every little thing becomes an annoying distraction. Ordinarily, these little annoyances would not arise, but under such circumstances discontent and repulsion bubble up spontaneously. On top of being annoyed, if you are under some kind of pressure, then you get into a frazzle both mentally and physically. Or, if you are not given the recognition or special treatment you think you deserve for your efforts, an unquiet feeling settles in your abdomen smoldering with malice.

Such things are disagreeable and painful for both yourself and others, and you yourself would probably just as well forget about them. But because these problems lie outside the realm of the intellect, they remain irresolvable by means of thought or reason. Since they lie outside the realm of intellect and reason, they are very difficult to deal with. This is especially true when some peculiar idea takes hold and doesn't let go.

A notion firmly planted in the head can be very difficult to get rid of. This is because the problem is related to the instinct for self-preservation. This instinct harbors a notion of some natural enemy and operates to affirm the predominance of the ego while at the same time denying recognition and acknowledgement of others. Anything planted in the mind in this way is not easily manageable because it involves an instinctive reaction to a threat on one's personal survival. This can arise from a voice or form of some kind that you encounter unexpectedly through circumstances you consider hostile. Therefore it is very difficult to deal with.

Right here is the real proof that joys and sorrows have no true form of their own. It is testimony that there is nothing in particular that can be regarded as the heart or mind. That such things can appear out of nowhere even though they don't exist in substance is evidence of the dreadful working of the ego.

What then is the mind of someone without an ego, of someone without ideas based on the self? It is the mind of the present moment now and of things simply or just as they are. It is the empty mind. It is the mind free from likes and dislikes, free from right and wrong, and unrestricted by personal opinions or feelings. It is the mind that has clarified the truth of non-substantiality. This state of mind is beyond being conceived by intellectual understanding, imagination, and so on. It is the mind where there is nothing and therefore is immutable. Simply speaking, this is called liberation or emancipation, but actually awakening for yourself is another matter. It can only be obtained by removing the gap between mind and body and realizing that originally both mind and body are one.

The reason for endeavoring in Zen practice is precisely for this reason. It is to simply and directly endeavor day and night in penetrating the present moment. Utterly and simply become the activity of the present moment. If you make effort diligently, your practice will deepen naturally, and the time will come when dropping off occurs. When you are really in search of the Way, you endeavor both day and night. No effort and pain can be spared. This is called "the Way-seeking Mind." This is the meaning of "...profoundly practicing Prajna Paramita."

### MU CHI YAKU MU TOKU I MU SHO TOKKO...

**"No wisdom and no attainment, because there is nothing to attain..."**

Concerning "No wisdom and no attainment," Shido Bunan comments, "In emptiness, there is no wisdom and no attainment." In regard to "nothing to attain," Bunan just says, "No need to repeat myself." When you have completely penetrated this world of things as they are, there is no wisdom or attainment because you realize nothing has existed from the beginning. Because everything is always full and complete, there is nothing at all to say or think or attain.

When you eat, you eat. When you walk, you walk. You do what you are doing now at the present moment. You pick up a bite of food with your chopsticks or fork and bring it to your mouth. You put it in your mouth and chew. This is truth itself; it is reality as it is. This is the Buddha Dharma. Right now, isn't this moment perfect and complete? What else could there be? Moreover, thinking there may be some special knowledge or thinking that there is something else to obtain is merely a personal view and a habit of the self. It is delusion, fantasy, and false perception. The purpose of Zen practice is to get rid of these habits of the self.

If you don't penetrate the present moment cutting off the habit of getting involved with arising thoughts, then you will always be tethered to flickering fragments of conscious and unconscious thoughts and feelings that bind you. This is what is referred to in Buddhism as being led astray. This is what Bunan is telling us to be especially careful about.

Whatever the circumstances, always diligently endeavor to just sit in Zazen and to just endeavor in your daily lives.

### BODAI SATTA E HANNYA HARAMITTA KO SHIN MUKEIGE...

**"Because the mind of the bodhisattva depends on Prajna Paramita, there are no obstacles..."**

A *bodhisattva* is someone who is on the path to Enlightenment. *Bodhi* and *Sattva* essentially have similar meanings. They signify awakening and reality. The mind of a bodhisattva is the Way-seeking Mind.

"There are no obstacles" means "I've removed the gap without any doubt and have become one with the present moment." This has come through "the deep practice of Prajna Paramita." Therefore obstacles no longer arise. Obstacles are the things that impede or disturb the mind. This means all things have become the original state of simply the thing itself without a single obstacle remaining.

The difference between the ancient masters and an unenlightened person is whether or not the gap between mind and body has been eliminated. In other words, the matter is whether or not there is a gap where thought can intervene, whether or not one is caught up in a continuum of mental activity, and whether or not a person perceives things in a self-other dualistic context. It is whether or not things are simply or just as they are. Does the self exist or not? Have you penetrated this matter or not? These questions are the same. Therefore, if you would just penetrate one of these questions, all questions will be resolved.

# MUKEIGE KO MU U FUKU...

*"Because there are no obstacles there is no fear..."*

Here it is needless to say more. If you drink water, your thirst will be quenched. When satisfied, there is no anxiety or discontent. Hence, to be fulfilled is called Nirvana. Fulfillment is when you have utterly become one with Zazen. It is when the self has disappeared. Since Zazen will prove this to you, you should simply and completely penetrate your Zazen practice.

## ONRI ISSAI TENDO MUSO KUGYO NEHAN...

*"Separate from everything, from upside-down thinking and from obtaining perfect enlightenment, too..."*

This phrase is a follow-up to the line at the beginning of the sutra, "...clearly realizing that the five skandhas are all empty, he was delivered from all suffering and pain." With this, everything was concluded. Upside-down thinking is the habit of being attached to 'names and forms,' 'words and concepts,' and thinking. However, when you penetrate the truth of the present moment, this habit ceases for good. Although Nirvana is ultimate and supreme, the truth of the present moment is both our original nature and something very ordinary. Nirvana is not something extraordinary. Therefore, it is only natural that both upside-down thinking and perfect enlightenment totally disappear. Reaching the true state of things simply as they are, you experience profound awakening.

When Dogen returned to Japan from China, he declared:

> I return empty-handed, without a trace of the Buddha Dharma. I simply realized that the eyes lie horizontal and the nose sits vertical. Every morning the sun rises from the east, and every evening the moon sinks in the west. Roosters crow in the early hours of the morning, and leap years arrive every four years.

Dogen became the state of things simply as they are and returned to Japan after wholeheartedly practicing for four years in China. He threw away everything, even the Buddha Dharma; therefore, there was nothing that even vaguely resembled the Buddha Dharma. He simply consented to the most ordinary fact that the eyes lie horizontal and the nose sits vertical. When morning comes, without fail the sun rises in the east, and every evening the moon sets in the west. Every four years is a leap year. This is true for past, present, and future. This is this, and that is that.

Zen master Mumon[27] said that in the study of Zen one should shun sound and form. He is saying that in Zen practice one should not be imprisoned by seeing, hearing, perceiving, and knowing. Forget mind and body; solely investigate and penetrate the present moment. Single-mindedly and utterly become the activity of this moment.

What's the inner meaning of penetrating this present moment that we call 'now'? What about you? If you are offered food, take food. If you are offered rice, receive rice. There is no other Dharma. Just investigate this.

---

27 Chinese Zen master who lived during the early 13th century.

# SANZE SHOBUTSU E HANNYA HARAMITTA KO TOKU A NOKU TARA SAN MYAKU SAN BODAI...

*"Because all of the Buddhas of the three realms depend on
Prajna Paramita, they reach perfect Enlightenment..."*

All of the Buddhas and Patriarchs of the three realms include: those of the past who dropped off mind and body and became one with things as they are; those of the present who have already become Buddhas; and those people practicing now in order to awaken in the future. "Because all of the Buddhas of the three realms depend on Prajna Paramita..." points to both the people who have already attained the Way and those who will attain it in the future. In other words, through Prajna Paramita they penetrate the present moment and attain the wisdom of supreme and perfect enlightenment.

A verse that is chanted during the ceremony for opening the *Perfection of Transcendent Wisdom* sutra says:

> *All things manifest due to cause and effect.*
> *Because of the law of cause and effect*
> *There is no coming and going.*
> *Because there is no coming and going*
> *There is no dwelling in the present.*

*Because there is no dwelling in the present*
*All things are void.*
*This is what is called Prajna Paramita.*

There is no truth, no Dharma, and no Enlightenment beyond this. "They reach perfect Enlightenment" means all of the bodhisattvas of the past, present, and future attain ultimate and true realization. Throwing away all vestiges of enlightenment, Great Enlightenment is achieved. In order to become like the patriarchs of the past you must forge and become intimate with your Zen practice just like the patriarchs did. If you become one with just the thing itself, you can become Buddha at any time.

The nun Myoshin was a disciple of Zen master Gyozan[28]. Once a group of 17 mendicant monks came from the region in China now known as Sichuan to meet Gyozan. Because it was evening when they arrived, Myoshin had them stay with her until morning. That evening the 17 monks were discussing the famous story of the Sixth Patriarch and the flag moving in the wind. Myoshin heard them speaking and said, "These 17 pathetic blind asses couldn't even begin to dream about the Buddha Dharma." When the monks from Sichuan heard that, they all became quiet and asked Myoshin about the Sixth Patriarch's true meaning. She told the monks to come closer. When they moved up to her, she said, "Neither the wind, nor the flag, nor the mind moves." With just this simple remark all 17 of the monks became enlightened because their practice had fully matured. Since they no longer had any need to meet Gyozan, they returned home. They all had attained supreme and perfect Enlightenment. This was due to Prajna Paramita.

Without a doubt, the 17 monks were able to awaken because they had thrown away everything and had simply walked during their long journey. They owe a great deal to simply walking. Kotei, a disciple of Zen master Tokusan, went to see his master. Tokusan stood on the other side the river at the water's edge and greeted him as he approached. Seeing Tokusan waving from across the river with his fan in hand Kotei experienced great Enlightenment. Everything was clarified at that moment. No longer having any need to meet with

---

28 Chinese Zen master who lived during the 9th century.

Tokusan, Kotei simply turned around and returned home. It was the result of his simply walking on his journey to visit his master.

The Buddha Way is right under your feet. When you reach the Way, you see it is right where you are. Attaining enlightenment you become complete. If you ceaselessly endeavor in preserving the present moment, awakening can occur anytime and anywhere because in the present moment 'now' the time is always ripe.

# KOCHI HANNYA HARAMITTA ZE DAIJIN SHU...

**"*Therefore you know. Prajna Paramita is the great holy mantra...*"**

"Therefore you know" means that you have mastered this without a doubt. You realize that Prajna Paramita is the supreme path and know that there could be no holier Way than this. *Holy* means free and unrestricted activity. The path of liberation is unrestricted and miraculous power.

A *mantra* is a sacred utterance, a request to be fulfilled. It is an appeal made when mind and body are one and thought and action are in harmony. In other words, it is a request that a prayer be answered. This is the meaning of "great holy mantra."

At last you are in complete accord with everything as it is. There is not the slightest particle of doubt. When standing or sitting, when seeing or hearing, the mind is simply functioning according to circumstances. You are free and unrestricted. In other words, nothing is as exalted as dropping off mind and body. Now this magnificent goal has been fulfilled.

Again, Shido Bunan sums this up saying, "Not worth mentioning." What he is saying is, "Now what kind of nonsense are you talking? From the beginning, an eye is an eye. A mountain is a mountain. Aren't the eyes horizontal and the nose vertical? How else could things be? Originally everything is perfectly settled. It is all completely out of our hands. That's all there is to it."

The underlying meaning here is if you don't really understand, you are just like a living corpse. That's why you have to penetrate the reality of the present moment. That is what Prajna Paramita is. If you attain liberation, you are free and unrestricted and can make use of this great treasure. It means to really penetrate this matter and to really awaken. The underlying spirit of these verses we have just been talking about is expressed throughout the sutra.

# ZE DAI JINSHU ZE DAI MYOSHU
# ZE MUJO SHU ZE MUTODO SHU...

*"This great holy mantra, this great bright mantra, this supreme mantra, this incomparable mantra..."*

This points to the unsurpassed and genuine awakening of "Supreme and Perfect Enlightenment," in other words, the dropping off of mind and body.

A monk asked Zen master Hyakujo[29], "What is something of marvelous wonder?"
Hyakujo said, "Sitting alone on Daiyu Peak."
The monk bowed.
Whereupon Hyakujo hit him.

This is from Case 26 of the *Blue Cliff Record*[30]. The monk who asked Hyakujo the question had some understanding of the Way and was trying to probe Hyakujo. "Master, I would like to ask you a question: What is the most miraculous thing in the world?" Pretending to understand nothing, the monk poses the question to Hyakujo. Something possessing phenomenal or superhuman ability wouldn't be called miraculous or wonderful because anything so phenomenal as to defy the law of cause and effect would not be real.

29  Chinese Zen master who lived during the 8th century.
30  A collection of Zen *koans* compiled in 11th century China.

Then what could truly be called "a marvelous wonder"?It would be to be the free and unrestricted use of the Dharma. It is the working of things just as they are.

Hyakujo's reply was simple:

*"sit-ting-a-lone-on-dai-yu-peak."*

He uttered it just as it is. There was just that, sound for sound, and nothing more. The words Hyakujo uttered may have sounded like doing Zazen "sitting alone on Daiyu Peak," but that was not his intended meaning. His mouth simply opened producing that utterance. This is exactly the same as Shakyamuni's holding up a flower and Makakasho smiling; it is the same as Tozan's "three pounds of flax"; it is Joshu's "mu" and also his famous "the oak tree in the garden"; it is Unmon's "shitstick." This reality is what became clear to the monk who was probing Hyakujo. His earnest prayer was fulfilled.

The monk simply heard Hyakujo's reply, and without any thought he simply bowed to Hyakujo. He respected Hyakujo. This monk had reached a degree of realization; there was no self and no Hyakujo. His action was spontaneous and unrestricted.

Hyakujo, too, without saying a word simply struck the monk. Transcending right and wrong there was nothing and no one. This is exactly like emptiness meeting emptiness. Since there is nothing, it is possible to become anything due on cause and effect. It means that the activity of simply doing and of simply being is a marvelous and extraordinary wonder. This is what the Dharma is.

For the bodhisattva Kannon, this marvelously wonderful matter now became clear. In other words, being completely liberated from all suffering and hardship, he joyfully announced the end of all suffering exclaiming, "Supreme Mantra," "Great Holy Mantra," "Great Bright Mantra," "Incomparable Mantra."

Here Shido Bunan remarks characteristically, "Not worth mentioning." What he means is that after realizing something so evident and natural, the bodhisattva shouldn't make a such fuss as if it were something new by going about shouting things like "great holy mantra" and "great bright mantra." Is it really something to be so excited by? The sun rises in the east and sets in the west. It really isn't anything moving or unusual. He should be ashamed that it has taken this long to wake up. He should just be quiet.

This is what deep compassion is. It is the same kind of compassion the Chinese Zen master Daie demonstrated when he burned the Blue Cliff Record[31].

Zen master Hakuin admonishes, "For your own sake, take a look again where you stand. Re-investigate and really get to the bottom of this matter." This is the same as Bunan's "words cannot reach." Buddha praises Prajna as the ultimate, but in Prajna where do you find superior and inferior? Gazing only upward at Prajna only offends it. Hakuin's admonition was for the sake of later generations, pointing out that the practice of investigating the present moment is itself "the great holy mantra," "the great bright mantra." That is what Prajna is. He is urging us to be aware and not to seek elsewhere.

Hakuin pompously tosses in, "I have no need for supreme wisdom." Instead of something so grand, Hakuin wants you to demonstrate without delay the lowliest form of Prajna. When you start chasing words and phrases, you corrupt Prajna. So in order to return to the Dharma's rightful teaching of suchness, of things as they are, Hakuin disposes of decorative phrases like "great holy mantra."

I would just like to remark that Hakuin's teacher, Shoju Ronin, was a disciple of Shido Bunan Zenji.

How would you answer Hakuin? In the reality of things as they are, there is no ultimate or highest, no second or third. There is no best or worst. Each and every thing is the whole universe. This is the supreme truth where there is no ultimate. Become the reality of things as they are. Become the thing itself.

*Incomparable* means no comparisons can be made. All things themselves are independent and unrivaled. When Buddha awakened, he proclaimed, "In all heaven and earth, I alone am the peerless one." Things are incomparable because no two things are alike in any respect. The Heart Sutra is a narrative extolling everything 'as it is'—each moment just as it is, each thing as it is. Everything is full and complete, and everyone stands on equal ground with the bodhisattva Kannon.

---

31 Because it apparently stimulated too much intellectual dialogue among his disciples.

# NOJO ISSAI KU...

*"Able to relieve all suffering..."*

This phrase is similar to the phrase that appears at the beginning of the sutra, "...delivered from all suffering and pain," affirming that liberation has been attained. From the beginning,

> Past mind cannot be grasped,
> Present mind cannot be grasped,
> Future mind cannot be grasped.

This means the bodhisattva Kannon truly understood there was no suffering, or anything else, which needed to be extinguished. It means that he penetrated the present moment and dropped off any notion of a self.

The next line of the sutra also emphasizes this point.

## SHIN JITSU FU KO...

*"This is true, not false..."*

In truth there are no impurities. Being genuine and unadulterated, truth is the reality of things just as they are. It is the fundamental character of the present moment. Eating is eating. Walking is walking. Zazen is Zazen. Water is water; water is not fire.

Things are not just devoid and meaningless. That is to say, things are always ample and full. In a text called *The Mind in Faith,* it is written, "No delusion to get rid of, no truth to seek." Also in it is, "There is no particular enlightenment, just give up personal opinions." These two passages mean there is nothing lacking and nothing extra. You must come to realize this well. If you penetrate the essential character of the present moment and awaken to the message and substance of no self, it will become clear that you have always been full and complete. Please investigate this matter for yourself.

# KO SETSU HANNYA HARAMITTA SHU SOKU SETSU SHU WATSU...

*"Therefore I proclaim the mantra of Prajna Paramita, proclaim the mantra that says..."*

The bodhisattva Kannon is saying, "Summing the matter up in this brief mantra, I proclaim the Prajna Paramita mantra. Expounding and clarifying this mantra, please grasp it well."

Things are already what they are. Rice is rice, and soup is soup. He is saying, "Firmly I take the bowl in hand, and unwaveringly I eat. This is Prajna Paramita. It is truth. I finally managed to reach the truth of the present moment. I've reached the end. Now I have gone beyond what should be done or attained and gone beyond what should be known. There is nothing more to be expounded or transmitted. Having utterly exhausted everything and removed all doubt, I have attained the immutable Great Teaching and accomplished the Buddha Way. There is not a single wasted word in the teaching of Buddha."

# GYATE GYATE HARA GYATE HARA SO GYATE...

Neither of the scholars Kumoraju nor Genjo Sanzo attempted to translate this phrase. The best way to convey its meaning was to leave it simply and directly as it originally was.

In the same way that *'caw caw'* is the sound of a crow cawing and *'woof woof'* the sound of a dog barking, the sound of the phrase, *'gya-te-gya-te-ha-ra-gya-te-ha-ra-so-gya-te,'* uttered simply 'as it is' is the best way to convey its original meaning. This really expresses the essence of the Heart Sutra as it is. Have you really clarified this vital matter for yourself? In other words, have you really awakened to the essential nature of the present moment for yourself?

In Sanskrit, *gyate* has two meanings: one is "depart," and other, "cross over." The principal meaning is something connected with the past. It means, "already the outcome." It means something that is finally carried through and settled. In other words, it means to be saved and liberated at long last. It means already one with things just as they are.

Shakyamuni Buddha said, "All sentient and insentient beings and myself together attain the Way; mountains, rivers, the grasses, and trees all realize Buddha together." It means the entire universe is from the same source, and all creation possesses the same nature. 'Self and other' has disappeared, and all things assimilate into oneness.

*Hara* of *hara gyate* means "to penetrate through," "to attain completely," or "to reach the source." It means awakening to the true present. It is ultimate reality.

*So* of *hara so gyate* means "universal," "all." The meaning is everyone and everything together awakens to Truth. All things are liberated.

The meaning of the entire expression is filled with such depth and magnitude that by itself it has become a mantra of mystical significance. This realization of Nirvana and liberation is something both inexpressible in words and impossible to understand. Consequently, in order to transmit its true meaning the scholar Sanzo decided to leave the phrase as it is. This was a magnificent way of clarifying both the means and outcome of Zen practice.

Finally we reach the last line.

## *BODAI SOWAKA HANNYA SHINGYO.*

*Bodai* is "Supreme Enlightenment," "the Way," "Truth." *sowaka* refers to arriving at universal truth, with a sense of having reached there swiftly, consummately, and directly. It is to penetrate the present moment, in other words, to reach Nirvana. Now it all becomes clear. It means mind and body drop away. It is the same as "this very mind itself is Buddha." The Heart Sutra expounds the True Way and presents the path to achieving it.

The meaning of the entire expression "*gyate gyate hara gyate hara so gyate bodai sowaka hannya shingyo*" is,

> "I finally penetrated and realized it. Gloriously everyone has accomplished it together. Assuredly, all have been saved and have attained liberation. Everyone together has arrived at Truth. Thus, the Way of Buddha has without a doubt been achieved. Rejoice, rejoice. Boundless Joy."

The true intent of Shakyamuni Buddha is to emancipate all people. The eighty-four thousand Dharma gates are for this reason. Furthermore, all of the ancient masters, all of the sutras, and all of the writings and teachings of the masters are for this reason. In brief, the Heart Sutra is an earnest appeal to penetrate "the deep practice of Prajna Paramita," which is the essential character of the present moment.

In *Bendowa*, an essay by Dogen, he writes, "All people are abundantly endowed with the Dharma. But if it is not practiced, it will not manifest. If it is not realized, it will not become your own." The outcome appears as a result of practice. Please investigate this great matter well.

Also in *Bendowa* he writes:

> The various Buddhas and Tathagatas all have the wondrous ability to attain the marvelous Dharma and Supreme Enlightenment. This is transmitted from Buddha to Buddha unconditionally through joyful Samadhi transcending all human contrivance. To become this Samadhi you must enter by means of the true gate of Zazen.

Zazen is Shikantaza. In this Zazen of simply sitting, where even the sitting itself is forgotten, there is no room for the discriminating mind to work. There is no space for any interference whatsoever in the functions of seeing, hearing, awareness, and knowing which manifest due to the activities of the six senses. When really absorbed in simply sitting, even the arising of fleeting thoughts does not distract you. Whatever your situation may be, forget mind and body, and devote yourself to Zazen practice be it day or night. At all times, simply devote yourself to the matter at hand. If you are wiping the floor, utterly devote your whole being to the activity to the extent that you and the task become one. Simply wipe the floor. Simply conduct yourself throughout the day. Let mind and body be one. The direct and unconditional gate to the Dharma is transmitted in this very way by the Buddhas and Patriarchs. "Look here! The eyes lie horizontal and the nose sits vertical." Is there anyone whose appearance is otherwise? Please investigate this matter thoroughly.

February 22, 2011

Rev. Kido Inoue, Abbot, Shorinkutsu Dojo
Takehara City, Hiroshima Prefecture, Japan
Age 71

# A DISCUSSION WITH KIDO INOUE ROSHI

## Questions of 4 practitioners

**Roshi:** You are all experienced and long-time sitters. During your time here you sat earnestly and intimately in your Zazen. However, it is regrettable that you now have to return home before you have the opportunity to completely penetrate it. In this way the seeds obstructing your practice appear before your Buddha Nature has the opportunity to manifest. Although this is truly regrettable, it is just how life is. This is why it sometimes takes so much time.

At first, we tend to become overanxious about things like Zen practice, the Dharma, and Enlightenment. If you are too anxious in your search for peace of mind, without realizing it you lose your direction, scavenging through words and expressions and clinging to personal ideas about the Dharma. Then your actual practice shows no improvement while pride in your intellectual understanding swells. But you should just sit, even if your condition is 'don't understand.' Whatever your condition may be, devote yourself exclusively to your breathing—inhaling and exhaling. When sitting, even if you become distracted and lose sight of your breathing, keep returning to it. Return to the breathing. If you faithfully endeavor in this way, you will come to realize in time how to ignore thinking and just practice Zazen and how to simply inhale and exhale, becoming one with the breathing alone.

Rigorously you have to become one with your breathing, brushing aside all thoughts. This is the meaning of expedient means 'as it is.' You should become the breathing exclusively. Then before long, distracted thinking subsides and you gradually become more comfortable and intimate with your mind and body. This is what is known as the virtue and merit of Zen practice.

**Practitioner A:** I am bothered by flickering thoughts arising and disappearing. But what I have come to notice is that I am able to recognize the moment when a thought arises. Just being able to do this I think is a clear milestone in my practice. When I practice 'just walking,' thoughts sometimes arise unexpectedly. But now I can immediately see how it disturbs my practice, and I immediately return to the present moment. Practice has become much easier because there is no longer any doubt about how to continue my practice. It is easier now that I am somehow more single-mindedly able to simply practice.

**Roshi:** You have obtained a degree of clarity, but you must persistently endeavor to deepen your practice.

**Practitioner A:** Forgive me for asking the same question time and again. But when walking, do you simply walk without paying attention to your breathing?

**Roshi:** Yes. When walking, simply walk. That is the Dharma. That is reality. If there is something extra you carry with you, or if your mind is elsewhere when you are just walking, then a gap arises and you separate yourself from the walking. You are unable to penetrate the present moment. Whatever the circumstances, simply devote yourself single-mindedly to becoming just the thing itself. What is essential here is to utterly become one with the thing itself. Without the slightest distraction simply do it. To become one with something means to penetrate it, to be entirely devoted to it.

**Practitioner A:** The best way to devote yourself to Zazen is to become single-mindedly and intently absorbed in 'simply sitting.' Isn't that right?

**Roshi:** Yes, exactly.

**Practitioner A:** For example, if you have a hundred people doing Zen practice, then naturally there would be 100 different ways of practicing. But the one thing common to them all would be the single-minded devotedness to this matter of 'simply' or 'just.' Isn't that right? The way one practices depends on the person, doesn't it? Some people walk quickly, some more slowly. Fast or slow is not the problem here. I think the only thing that matters is becoming just the thing itself where there is no room for thoughts to enter. Isn't that right?

**Roshi:** That is exactly right. When you have thoroughly penetrated that, it is called awakening, or *kensho*.

**Practitioner A:** Is the conflict that arises between religions due to the diverging differences in fundamental beliefs between them? For example, instead of endeavoring single-mindedly in an effort to forget the ego, perhaps one believes in and strives to find some imagined ideal.

**Roshi:** I think so. Believing in God or Buddha is very important because it indicates an existence that has penetrated and seen through man's torment and wickedness. The fear of divine punishment or god's wrath keeps man's heart and mind from getting out of control. However, a person's fixed and deep-seated personal views are rooted in the ego. Because of this, humankind is saddled with karmic hindrance created from past deeds and is afflicted by the three poisons of greed, anger, and foolishness. Any system of beliefs that doesn't recognize such a danger ignores the seeds of humankind's afflictions.

A true religion awakens people to the fact that the root of all evil lies in the self. But that is not enough. A true religion provides the concrete measures and means to clearly resolve this matter of the ego. Such a religion can be called the Path, the Law, or the Dharma. The person with fixed and deep-seated personal beliefs often harbors a sense of hostility for views conflicting with his or her own. It is difficult for such a person to escape confrontation. Moreover, if you look closely, you can often find the seeds for cruelty in the hearts of such people.

There is no way that God could calmly create a holocaust just for having his trust betrayed. But when authority and power get tied up in religious beliefs, mankind has no qualms about openly performing the most beastly acts, even things more inhumane and unjust than wars. This is what heresy is. If you look back through history, you can easily understand this. It is something we have to be especially careful about.

The practice of the Buddha Way is not about beliefs. It is about throwing away mind and body and becoming one with the present moment. This is the main focus and the entire teaching of Buddhism. If you can firmly understand this, you will not lose sight of the way to practice. This is because you will possess the conviction that you only have to be focused on here and now, becoming one with the present moment without looking elsewhere.

**Practitioner A:** In other words, it is the belief in a self which is the basic factor that creates the mistaken view of the separation between mind and body. Is that right? When you penetrate this matter and the ego drops off, the gap disappears and mind and body become one. At this time, past mental and physical habits of clinging to our mind and body will disappear. Then reality will clearly manifest itself and the individual will be liberated. Is this how we should understand what you are saying?

**Roshi:** That is exactly right.

**Practitioner A:** Thank you. Now I understand the consequences of harboring beliefs and convictions that are based on the self. One has to get rid of the self that harbors these beliefs. Now I see more clearly the purpose for doing Zen practice. Thank you very much.

**Roshi:** The effort to completely throw away the self is called the practice of the Buddha Way. In this way these habits of the mind are resolved, and as a result he or she is liberated. Becoming one is the way to awakening to that boundless world.

[During a sitting period of Zazen, a practitioner named Mr. Komori became the sitting itself. There was just the sitting, nothing else. Roshi noticed this. He quickly walked over to where Mr. Komori was sitting and yelled, "Katsu!" Mr. Komori simply raised his hand slowly and waved it.]

**Roshi:** If there is anyone here who clearly understands his present state, please speak up and tell us.

**Practitioner A:** His present state is no self and no other. It is just as it is.

**Roshi:** Good! He is truly and simply sitting. It is just as you see. No words are needed. It is just as it is without any room for words. Here is the important point of practice. This is how you should practice every day, always being in the present moment without being distracted.

**Practitioner B:** About his present state of mind, do you practice continuing in this way today, tomorrow, the next day, and so on?

**Roshi:** Does the present moment continue into the future? What do you think?

**Practitioner B:** The present is the present, but it cannot be grasped.

**Roshi:** That's right. Concerning your question about his practice continuing or not, you understand that this mind cannot be grasped, don't you?

**Practitioner B:** Yes.

**Roshi:** Yes, but because something suits us or because it feels good, we wish and strive for the thing to continue. Such things are merely concerns of the ego. They are delusion, fantasy, and false perception. In short, they are attachments. The practice of the Buddha Way is to resolve the habit of seeking such delusions, fantasies, and apparitions. Just become this present moment we call 'now.' But unless you have penetrated to the source, the habits of the mind will never fall way. Therefore you must never be negligent in your practice.

**Practitioner B:** Thank you. In other words, endeavor to become absolutely one with the present moment. Zen practice is throwing away thoughts and intentions and becoming intimate with the present moment.

**Roshi:** Exactly. It is to endeavor earnestly in becoming one with the present circumstances without being distracted by unnecessary thinking. This is the meaning of expedient means just as they are. It is just this moment as it is.

**Practitioner B:** Now I understand. Since all things are made up of causal factors, simply becoming one with the reality of the present moment just as it is what Zen practice is.

**Roshi:** Good! This matter of 'simply' demonstrates cause and effect as it is. In things as they are, there is no good or bad, no excess or lack, therefore it is always just right. This is what is called paradise or bliss.

Here I've just mentioned about paradise, I would like to say a few more words about it. We usually think of paradise as some sort of utopian dream where all of our wants are fulfilled without effort, suffering, or perseverance. But if you really lived like that, this kind of paradise would actually be hell. There would be no law of cause and effect; therefore, everything would fall into chaos. Even apart from chaos, the boredom and sense of emptiness would be overwhelming. Why? Because you would always be full without being fulfilled. In order to eat, your stomach has to be empty. If you were always granted what you want, you would not be able to give full play to your aspirations or lofty ideals, and you would be unable to test or demonstrate your abilities or skills. You would be unable to savor things. You would lose your reason to live.

In order to attempt new things or to bring out your abilities certain conditions are needed. There is delight in making possible what is impossible. The pursuit and perseverance needed to bring something to fruit arise from aspirations and ideals. Since you never know what is going to happen, a measure of caution is needed; but it has to be done in an environment of perseverance, compromise, resoluteness, and pain. These are the conditions needed to create an environment where reaching fulfillment is possible. This is really the only way to live. Under these conditions we become one with circumstances and forget the self. This is the true meaning of paradise.

Therefore paradise is not "over there" on the other shore. It is you yourself, your present condition exactly as it is now. The moment you fantasize and dream about some kind of utopian illusion you lose the present moment and fall into hell. At the same time, though, it can also be said that paradise is residing peacefully in hell. Paradise and utopia are what you make them. You must only awaken to this fact. The six realms of existence include: heaven, earth, hell, hungry ghosts, brutes, and fighting devils. The reason why heaven is an illusionary world is because any world where everything is good is just a world of fantasy. Do not mistakenly think that heaven is the world of satori or enlightenment.

The present environment for raising children is terribly inadequate. Since children are given most of the material things they want, they are not taught such qualities as endeavor, patience, and tolerance. In other words, they lack what is needed for fostering the ability to reach their own happiness: they lack the ability to endeavor. Real learning comes from imagining and creating; it comes from imitating and falling on your face in failure. A sense of accomplishment cannot be learned or acquired from someone else. It is playing the game in earnest. It is enduring. It is working up a sweat. The only one who can savor these things is you yourself. You yourself are the only one who can do this. A parent shows a child how to do it, and then the child tries for him or herself. Here the parent fosters the spirit of always doing your best whatever the circumstances may be. Under circumstances like these, a child can be raised properly.

These are sound principles for living your life properly. So I would hope that religious leaders, educators, parents, and all members of society would pay closer attention to fundamental factors concerning the raising of our children. They are the caretakers of the future.

**Practitioner B:** I have never heard anybody talk about the Dharma like this before. The focus of Zen practice is much clearer now. I understand much better. I see now that living peacefully in the present is to become the present moment and that to penetrate the present reality is what paradise really is.

**Roshi:** Just leave everything up to cause and effect, and don't be distracted by things. That is what Zen practice is. That is all it is. This is what 'simply' means. Paradise is the world of 'simply,' the world of things simply and just as they are.

**Practitioner C:** I see now.

**Roshi:** If you don't really penetrate this, you will never know what true satisfaction is. The reason why it becomes yours once you've penetrated it is because the self, which is unable to grasp or comprehend this matter, melts away and vanishes. In short, all suspicions and debate disappear; therefore, you naturally live peacefully.

**Practitioner C:** I thought so. Asking yourself "why" is also delusion and fantasy. It only means the self is getting involved.

**Roshi:** That's exactly right. The mental activity surrounding the question of why provides the seeds for doubt and deliberation. Therefore, if thought, consideration, consciousness, conception, and ideas are not left as they are, the habit of the mind of continually linking thoughts one after the other will never be resolved.

**Practitioner C:** I think that in order to get rid of this habit of the mind, no matter what doubts may arise we should ignore them and simply endeavor in the present moment.

**Roshi:** That's right. Whether it is Buddha or your parents, or whatever, they are all delusion. True practice of the Buddha Way is to endeavor to throw away all things. There is only one vital principle and that is to devote yourself exclusively to utterly becoming one. Everything else must be completely thrown away. Completely throwing away everything is what "penetrating to the bottom" means. In other words, it means to forget the ego.

**Practitioner C:** I see now. Thank you.

**Practitioner B:** Please explain to us about the proper way to eat.

**Roshi:** Simply and single-mindedly eat without being distracted. Don't eat ravenously like some animal. Really eat earnestly one bite at a time. That is what being one with the moment is. The essential point of practice is to harmonize mind and body and to completely awaken to Supreme Enlightenment. It is to simply and single-mindedly do the thing. Therefore, while chewing your food, don't thoughtlessly fidget with your chopsticks or fork. When chewing, there is only chewing; therefore, you should do only that. In other words, be single-minded. When you endeavor like this, you can rectify crude and inattentive behavior patterns that you unconsciously carry out. A dramatic change takes place at the root of consciousness.

The essential point is to single-mindedly eat: be in the present moment. You straighten out inattentive eating habits by simply and mindfully eating. Frankly speaking, if you are unable to properly do something as simple as eating a meal, you don't have any business talking about Zen.

**Practitioner D:** In other words, not just when eating, but in everything we do we should give it our utmost attention and simply do it. Is that right?

**Roshi:** Yes. Whatever you are doing, without thinking, just be one with the very moment. All things are essentially the Way. Therefore if you endeavor simply and honestly, the Way will naturally unfold for you. Mind is one; therefore, in whatever you do, if you do it single-mindedly, you can reach your goal.

**Practitioner B:** It just means to heed the teaching and to practice it faithfully and earnestly. Is that right?

**Roshi:** That's right. Believe the teaching and practice it straightforwardly and honestly. This may sound rather unequivocal, but there is actually no other way.

It is the same as in medicine, sports, or any other field. In order to study and master something, you have to follow a teacher you believe in and you must endeavor according to the teaching. In order to practice the Way you have to do it with abandon. If you are really earnest about it, you must study under a true teacher. The only real way to lead someone to awakening is to tell them exactly what must be done and not beat around the bush. It is up to the student to just carry it through. Therefore, in regard to the Way, the more severe the teacher is the better.

**Practitioner D:** You mean you really have to throw your whole self into it.

**Roshi:** That's right. From the beginning there is no self; therefore, it takes devoted and wholehearted effort in order to forget the habits of the self. In other words, become like a fool; simply and honestly practice the Way. Even doing so, the self still becomes a hindrance making it difficult to really become the kind of fool needed to practice.

Since it is a matter of simply doing, you might say there couldn't be anything easier. Therefore, it is the empty-headed fool who is actually a sage or saint. The mind of a sage, or a holy person, is the state of no-mind, where no falsehood exists.

**Practitioner D:** To be a great fool is to single-mindedly be one with the present moment. Is that what a sage is?

**Roshi:** That's right.

**Practitioner D:** Forgive me for repeatedly asking. Ultimately, is reality just the present moment? In order to realize this, you become intimate with the present moment? Once you have really penetrated this, you are liberated? Does that about sum it up? You become a great fool?

**Roshi:** Yes, exactly. When you penetrate this, the proof will manifest itself. It will become self-evident. This is the heart and substance of the Buddha Dharma.

However, if any trace of 'now' or shadow of 'simply' remains, then you haven't completely penetrated to the bottom. It is not liberation. Therefore you must be aware that a person with a shallow grasp of the present moment can only attain a shallow grasp of the Dharma. Everything begins now and ends now; therefore, no matter how you look at it, 'now' is everything. In other words, this matter of 'as it is' is the beginningless and endless present moment. When you have realized this, you awaken to the peacefulness of Nirvana that is called Buddha.

What is important is the actual personal proof obtained by really penetrating the present moment and becoming one with the thing itself. If there is no definitive great awakening, there will be no true settlement or resolution. At any rate, just become a great fool and penetrate this matter.

**Practitioner D:** As children, I believe we acted in such a way.

**Roshi:** Yes, that's right. When children play, they become fully absorbed in what they are doing. Just taking things as they come, they forget everything else and are immersed in what they are doing. Nevertheless, they are happy with that. That is important. It is the mind of non-discrimination.

But the reason why they don't become enlightened is they haven't penetrated thoroughly enough to awaken a determinative self-awareness that the ego has dropped off. And so it only lasts while they are playing, and afterwards they return to the dualistic world. It ends without an awakening experience.

If you do not really penetrate and realize for yourself that hot is hot and cold is cold, you will never understand that it is attachments that bind you. You will be unable to break through the habits of the ego self. There is the story of a monkey who loses his life grasping at the moon's reflection in a pool of water. That is how monkeys act.

It is because of the mind that a person is able to realize his or her true nature and can throw away the self. It is due to the mind that people can experience both delusion and enlightenment. It is by somehow giving up this mind that we are able to become bodhisattvas and Buddhas. At the same time, it is by that same mind that through endeavor anybody can awaken to their true selves. I hope you can now understand the reason why "this very mind is Buddha."

**Host:** Our time is over. This discussion about the teaching of the Dharma was very valuable for all of us. Thank you very much.

# CONTACT ADDRESS

Shorinkutu Dojo, 2-10-1 Tadanoumi-tokonoura
Takehara-shi Hiroshimaken, zip 729-2314, Japan
Tel. 81-846-26-1264
Fax. 81-846-26-0565
URL: http://www.geocities.jp/shorinkutu/
E-mail: shorinkutu@ybb.ne.jp